Freudulent Encounters

(for the Jung at Heart)

Still More Readings from the *Journal of Polymorphous Perversity*®

edited by

Glenn C. Ellenbogen, Ph.D.

W. W. Norton & Company   New York   London

To three very supportive friends:
Chris Holle, Suzi Tucker, and Ilene Bernstein

Crazy for Loving You: Notes From Week One of the Psychiatrists' Strike © 1991 James Gorman. Originally in *The New Yorker*. Reprinted by permission.

My Life: A Series of Privately Funded Performance-Art Pieces © 1990 Susan Orlean. Originally in *The New Yorker*. Reprinted by permission.

All other selections © 1989, 1990, 1991, 1992, Wry-Bred Press, Inc.

The name *Journal of Polymorphous Perversity* is a Registered Trademark under exclusive license to Wry-Bred Press, Inc.

The material appearing in this book originally appeared in the *Journal of Polymorphous Perversity*®, a humor magazine available by subscription from Wry-Bred Press, Inc., P.O. Box 1454, Madison Square Station, New York, NY 10159-1454.

Freudulent Encounters (for the Jung at Heart): Still More Readings from the *Journal of Polymorphous Perversity*® © 1992 Wry-Bred Press, Inc. All rights reserved.

First Edition

The text of this book is composed in Times Roman. Composition and manufacturing by The Maple-Vail Book Manufacturing Group.

Library of Congress Cataloging-in-Publication Data

Freudulent encounters (for the Jung at Heart) : still more readings from the Journal of polymorphous perversity / edited by Glenn C. Ellenbogen.
  p. cm.
  1. Psychiatry—Humor. 2. Psychology—Humor. I. Ellenbogen.
Glenn C. II. Journal of polymorphous perversity.
PN6231.P785F74 1992
150'.207—dc20   92–9217

ISBN 0-393-03422-4

W. W. Norton & Company, Inc., 500 Fifth Avenue, New York, N.Y. 10110
W. W. Norton & Company Ltd., 10 Coptic Street, London WC1A 1PU

1 2 3 4 5 6 7 8 9 0

Contents

Chapter 8 **Experimental Psychology**

Preface

WHEN I ENTERED graduate school in the mid-70s to pursue a Ph.D. in clinical psychology, I was looking forward to getting a good education in human behavior. I soon discovered one critical human quality particularly lacking in (and certainly unappreciated by) those in the mental health field: a sense of humor.

As I progressed through coursework, practicums, internships, and the doctoral dissertation—the last involving a process that I affectionately came to call "the primal hump"—I began to see how humor could serve the healthy purpose of helping one keep perspective on Life. The most important thing I learned in graduate school, then was that developing and nurturing a sense of humor is essential for maintaining perspective and mental health.

Of course, I was not the first to see a relationship between humor and health. Norman Cousins showed that humor could have a significant impact on one's physical well-being. My experiences in graduate school reinforced for me that humor could have a powerful impact on one's mental well-being as well.

Eager to make it through graduate school with some degree of sanity, I began writing spoofs of psychology (touching on topics ranging from the missing "nasal stage" in Freudian theory to the uncanny parallels between contemporary diagnostic practices in psychology and colonial New England's Salem Witchcraft Trials). It worked: I earned my Ph.D. and remained relatively sane.

In 1980, armed with my newly won Ph.D., I sat down and wrote a lampoon of the most sophisticated intelligence test ever devised, calling my test "The Scale of Mental Abilities Requiring Thinking Somewhat" (S.M.A.R.T.S.). At the same time, I founded a small publishing house—Wry-Bred Press—to produce and distribute spoofs of psychology. The S.M.A.R.T.S. test was published as a "monograph" under the banner of the *Journal of Polymorphous Perversity,* a fictitious periodical. As this monograph slowly made its way into the field, I began receiving not only letters of encouragement from psychologists, psychiatrists, and other mental health professionals, but humorous submissions "for consideration by your journal" as well. I found this course of events funny in and of itself: I was receiving submissions to a periodical that did not even exist. Clearly, the message was that the field was in desperate need of some lightening up.

In response to the positive feedback, I began laying the groundwork for the launching of a real journal. On January 2, 1984, the first issue of the *Journal of Polymorphous Perversity* was published. The lead article? "Psychotherapy of the Dead."

Initially, the reception was quite mixed. Marketing a spoof of psychology to a group of seemingly serious, sober, sometimes even somber, mental health professionals was no easy task. In fact, there was one group of mental health professionals—the strict, orthodox Freudians of the American Psychoanalytic Association—that outright banned the display of the *Journal of Polymorphous Perversity* at their annual convention, declaring that humor was "inappropriate." The other two "APAs"—the American Psychological Association and the American Psychiatric Association—readily permitted the magazine to be exhibited at their conventions. The general public seemed to respond more positively (less defensively?) to the spoofs and a sizable number of non-mental health professionals made up the first year's subscription roster.

As issues of the *Journal of Polymorphous Perversity* continued to hit the field, I began to see signs that the magazine was starting to have an impact on psychology. Invitations to address state and regional psychological associations on the topic of humor and psychology began to come in. Reprints of journal articles began creeping their way into introductory psychology textbooks. Finally, one of the leading publishers of *serious* scholarly/professional psychology texts invited me to put together an anthology.

In 1986, *Oral Sadism and the Vegetarian Personality* was published. The publisher had taken a courageous gamble not only in publishing its first humor book, but in publishing one that satirized its bread and butter. To the publisher's relief, the book was accepted (if not embraced) by a psychological community long-accustomed to consuming dry, serious, oftentimes pedantic psychological works. *Oral Sadism and the Vegetarian Personality* became one of the company's bestsellers, eventually published in both German and Japanese. In 1989, a second anthology—*The Primal Whimper*—was published by another company to an equally warm reception.

Which brings us to 1992. Certainly, the *Journal of Polymorphous Perversity* has made some inroads in helping mental health professionals to become less serious, to take humor more seriously. But, there's more work to be done. It's time, once again, for an assault on the stuffy, the stodgy, and the stoic. *Freudulent Encounters (for the Jung at Heart)* is a fresh attack.

Glenn C. Ellenbogen
New York, New York

Acknowledgments

I WOULD LIKE to gratefully acknowledge the help of the following *Journal of Polymorphous Perversity*® associate editors, who were kind enough to review manuscripts that touched upon their speciality areas:

Milton Spett, Ph.D. (Clinical Psychology), Edward E. Coons, Ph.D. (Comparative/Physiological Psychology), Gregory N. Reising, Ph.D. (Counseling Psychology), Les Halpert, Ph.D. (Developmental Psychology), George E. Rowland, Ph.D. (Engineering Psychology), Richard J. Koppenaal, Ph.D. (Experimental Psychology), James F. Harper, Ph.D. (Forensic Psychology), Robert Perloff, Ph.D. (Industrial Psychology), Gordon D. Wolf, Ph.D. (Medical Psychology), Charles F. Levinthal, Ph.D. (Neuropsychology), Chris Holle, M.S.N. (Psychiatric Nursing), Benjamin Strouse, M.S.W. (Psychiatric Social Work), Robert S. Hoffman, M.D. (Psychiatry and Neurology), Estelle Wade, Ph.D. (Psychoanalysis), Hilary James Liberty, Ph.D. (Statistics), David O. Herman, Ph.D. (Test and Measurements).

As the definition of what constitutes "good" humor is very subjective, the associate editors were rarely in agreement, either among themselves or with me, about which articles merited publication. The responsibility for making the final selections for the regular journal issues and for this anthology was ultimately mine and mine alone. The presence of any given article in this anthology should not be construed as reflecting the endorsement of the associate editors.

Finally, I would like to thank the many authors whose works appear in this anthology.

1

Psychotherapy

Franchising Unorthodox, Eclectic Psychotherapeutic Services: Psychotherapists-R-Us

Keith Humphreys

University of Illinois at Champaign-Urbana

THE FACT THAT TRADITIONAL psychotherapy is not appropriate for all clients is made no clearer than in Freud's now famous case of Wilhelmina K. Wilhelmina had entered into a five-day-a-week analysis and, despite expert application of psychoanalytic techniques by Freud, shared nothing of her current life or childhood memories. It was not until Wilhelmina's sister arrived one day to pick her up after therapy that Freud learned that Wilhelmina was not resistant but a deaf-mute, and that she was laboring under the misapprehension that Freud was also. In retrospect, Freud saw that Wilhelmina's hand gestures—one in particular— had been attempts at communication. Wilhelmina and her sister left Freud's office in a Huff (a very popular car in those days) and were never seen again. In later years, Freud would relate this anecdote to his students along with the important lesson it had taught him: When a patient is difficult or temperamental, *always* insist on payment in advance.

At franchised Psychotherapists-R-Us Centers, we administer unorthodox treatment to the Wilhelminas of the world. Psychotherapists-R-Us staff members conduct treatment from a variety of theoretical and sexual orientations, but the unifying ideology of the centers is unconditional, nonjudgmental acceptance of any major credit card. While our application of scientific principles is not particularly rigorous or demanding, we more than make up for this laxness in our stringent billing and collection policies. As it is far easier to convey the atmosphere of the Psychotherapists-R-Us Centers through case histories than a global overview, several choice cases have been selected from our files for presentation. In accordance with Psychotherapists-R-Us ethical standards, all diagnoses were randomly assigned and client names were changed to those of people who have posed billing problems in recent weeks.

Case 1: The Obsessive-Compulsive Accountant

Mr. David Nefler was a nervous-looking accountant who impressed the intake worker as being extremely tall for a man of his height. Mr. Nefler was plagued by a constant obsession that he had been jilted by the Vice President of the United States, which compelled him to send the Veep numerous touching love letters. It was of little consolation to Mr. Nefler that the majority of letters met with only lukewarm replies, although at a bad time in the VP's marriage there was a hint that "something might be worked out after the upcoming primaries."

Mr. Nefler's obsessions, annoying attention to detail, and inability to relax and enjoy life warranted the diagnosis of Obsessive Compulsive Disorder (OCD). As treatment, 5 years of milieu therapy in a clinical psychology graduate program was applied with positive results, as the OCD transmuted into PhD, a more intractable but socially acceptable disorder.

Case 2: The Rich Man With No Real Problems

Warren Cremer was a multimillionaire who presented at the Psychotherapists-R-Us Center for directions to the Champaign Country Club. He appeared to be well functioning, but his huge income in combination with our budget crunch dictated that a lengthy and expensive treatment be initiated. Mr. Cremer was assigned to our special inverted group therapy, in which one patient facilitates a group for eight psychotherapists, all of whom are paid hourly. Outcome of treatment was excellent, resulting in complete remission and a new leather couch for our waiting room.

LIMITED PROSPECTUS

Psychotherapists-R-Us franchises are still available but going fast, so take this opportunity to get in on the ground floor of this exciting, rewarding, and lucrative therapy business. For a one-time fee of just $20,000 plus 7% of your annual gross sales, we provide you with all that you need: billing forms, one copy of the DSM-III-R, a display advertisement for Psychotherapists-R-Us (just fill in your local franchise address!), malpractice insurance application forms, and an intensive, 90-minute training course for your staff on theories and techniques of therapeutic intervention. Sign up today and we'll send you enough free "I'VE BEEN IN THERAPY SO LONG, I'VE BEGUN TO SEE GROWTH IN MY THERAPIST" bumper stickers for every member of your staff. Address all franchise applications and inquiries to the author c/o Psychotherapists-R-Us Centers World Headquarters, Box 20000+7, Champaign, IL 61820.

Psychiatrist Surname and the Presenting Problems of Psychotherapy Patients: Implications for Treatment and Therapy Outcome

Ernst von Krankman, Ph.D.

IN HIS SEMINAL, penetrating, heuristic, parsimonious, cogent, insightful, ground-breaking, advanced, up-to-date, and well-written, paper, von Krankman (1989) performed an "exhaustive, not to mention exhausting search" of the 70,000 surnames of psychologists listed in the official membership register of the American Psychological Association, in order to identify those key surnames of psychologists that might be indicated or contraindicated in working with psychotherapy patients with specific diagnostic presenting problems. Von Krankman demonstrated, for example, that psychologists with the name "Dr. Balance" might be indicated (or +) for patients who are manic-depressives, whereas psychologists with the name "Dr. Bolt" might be contraindicated (or −) for those who have had negative experiences with ECT. And then there were those really tough diagnostic judgment calls, where it was unclear whether a psychologist's surname was indicated or contraindicated. Patients who are perfectionistic, for instance, might be eager to enter treatment with a psychologist named "Dr. Toogood," although it is unclear (or ?) whether this would be truly therapeutic for them. In concluding, von Krankman called for researchers to continue his pioneering work by investigating the surnames of other mental health professionals. In keeping with von Krankman's noble research goals, the present author (von Krankman) conducted an equally exhaustive and exhausting investigation, only this time of the surnames of psychiatrists listed in the 1,941 pages of the American Psychiatric Association's Biographical Directory (1989). The resultant data are presented below.

6

Psychiatrist's Surname	Indication	Diagnostic Presenting Problem
Dr. Akin *also* Dr. Akins	?	Patients with incestuous backgrounds
Dr. Amaker	?	B, C, and D students
Dr. Asch *also* Dr. Ascher *also* Dr. Ascherman *also* Dr. Ash *also* Dr. Asher *also* Dr. Ashman	?	Fire setters
Dr. Askew	—	Patients with reality testing problems
Dr. Backup	? ?	Anal-retentive patients Patients who work with computers
Dr. Balasubramanian	—	Learning disabled patients
Dr. Bark *also* Dr. Barker	?	Patients with Tourette's disorder
Dr. Beebee	—	Stutterers
Dr. Beitman	?	Oral-aggressive and oral-sadistic patients
Dr. Blackmore	—	Depressives
Dr. Blazer	?	Fire setters
Dr. Blinder	?	Hysterical conversion disorders
Dr. Bookspan	?	Patients with memory problems
Dr. Bralove	?	Female patients concerned with breast size
Dr. Braverman	?	Competitive patients

(continued)

Psychiatrist's Surname	Indication	Diagnostic Presenting Problem
Dr. Brightwell	+	Depressives
	?	Manics
Dr. Broadway	?	Histrionic patients
	?	Narcissistic patients
Dr. Buck *also* Dr. Buckman	−	Patients who feel that others are not really interested in them for who they really are, rather for what they can gain from them
Dr. Bunney *also* Dr. Burdi	?	Regressed patients
Dr. Butcher	−	Any patient (with the exception of those employed in the meat industry)
Dr. Carlock *also* Dr. Carraway	?	Sociopathic patients with a history of auto theft
Dr. Carvell	?	Anorectics
	?	Bulimics
Dr. Circle	?	Obsessive-compulsives
Dr. Cleaver	?	Adolescents who have experienced acute psychotic breaks after watching *Friday the 13th* (Part 1 through 100)
Dr. Colon	?	Anal-retentive patients
	+	Grammarian patients
Dr. Conway *also* Dr. Conwell	?	Sociopaths
Dr. Converse	?	Teenage patients obsessed with status footwear
Dr. Copeland	+	Patients with poor impulse control

(continued)

Psychiatrist's Surname	Indication	Diagnostic Presenting Problem
Dr. Croissant	?	French bulimics
Dr. Crowder	−	Claustrophobic patients
Dr. Crummie	?	Inarticulate, acting-out teenagers
Dr. Cutter	−	Patients with castration anxiety
Dr. Dank	?	Enuretics
Dr. De Bolt *also* Dr. De Fries	−	Patients with a history of ECT treatment
Dr. De John	?	Female prostitute patients
Dr. De Long	?	Patients concerned with penis size
Dr. De Witt	?	Manics
Dr. Dearman	+	All patients
Dr. Dim	− ?	Depressives Patients with IQs between 70 and 79 (borderline retardates)
Dr. Dollar	−	*See* Dr. Buck
Dr. Dredge	?	Psychoanalytic patients
Dr. Falick *also* Dr. Fallick	?	Patients obsessed with sexuality
Dr. Fetter	?	Patients invested in bondage and dominance
Dr. Finder	+ + +	Amnesiacs Patients with senile dementia Patients with dissociative states
Dr. Fineman	+	All patients

(continued)

Psychiatrist's Surname	Indication	Diagnostic Presenting Problem
Dr. First	?	Competitive patients
	?	Yuppie patients
Dr. Forgotson	?	Male patients neglected by their fathers
Dr. Fullilove	?	Nymphomaniacs
Dr. Gabby *also* Dr. Gaby	?	Manic patients
Dr. Garb *also* Dr. Garber	?	Shopping addicted patients
Dr. Go	+	Agoraphobics
Dr. Gross *also* Dr. Grosser *also* Dr. Grossman *also* Dr. Grossmann	?	Adolescent patients
Dr. Guterman *also* Dr. Gutterman	?	Alcoholic patients who have hit rockbottom
Dr. Ha	?	Defiant adolescent patients
Dr. Hardaway	–	Impotent patients
Dr. Hatcher	?	Pregnant patients ambivalent about having children
Dr. Hoover	?	Compulsive cleaners
Dr. Hu	–	Learning disabled patients unable to spell "Who"
Dr. Hug	+	Patients who have difficulty with intimacy and closeness
	+	All other patients

(continued)

	Psychiatrist's Surname	Indication	Diagnostic Presenting Problem
49	Dr. Inbody	–	Delusional patients experiencing themselves as possessed
50	Dr. Jeckel	?	Patients with rapid and unpredictable mood swings
51	Dr. Jurka	?	Acting-out, Italian-born patients who still speak with Italian accents
52	Dr. Kaak	+	Learning disabled patients who see and spell words backwards
53	Dr. Kilburn	?	Sociopathic firesetters
54	Dr. Kind *also* Dr. Kinder	+	All patients
55	Dr. Koutsogiannopoulos	–	*See* Dr. Balasubramanian
56	Dr. Kowatch	?	Identical twins remanded for therapy following incident of voyeurism
57	Dr. Kwit	?	Patients with a long history of dropping out of therapy
58		?	Patients with poor frustration tolerance
59	Dr. Livingood	?	Economically deprived, acting-out, inner-city youths oriented toward materialistic goals, remanded to therapy
60	Dr. Liverman	?	Alcoholic patients
61	Dr. Llewellyn	–	Stutterers
62	Dr. Mac Lean	?	Anorectics of Scottish descent
63			*(continued)*

Psychiatrist's Surname	Indication	Diagnostic Presenting Problem
Dr. Maddock	−	Patients concerned about the mental health of their doctor
Dr. Mars	−	Patients experiencing everyone around them as foreign and strange
Dr. Mateus	?	Alcoholic patients
Dr. Mellow	+	All patients
Dr. Moon	−	*See* Dr. Mars
also Dr. Mooney	?	Patients who are/have been members of cults
Dr. Moss *also* Dr. Mossman	−	Catatonic patients
Dr. Nix *also* Dr. Nunn	?	Negativistic patients
Dr. Noshpitz	?	Eating disordered patients
Dr. Nudelman	?	Intellectualized patients
Dr. Oder	−	Patients suffering from olfactory hallucinations
Dr. Oh	?	Patients having difficulty expressing strong feelings
Dr. Oko	+	*See* Dr. Kaak
Dr. O'Lone	?	Avoidant personality disorders
Dr. Owings	?	Compulsive gamblers in debt
Dr. Pettipiece	−	Patients concerned with penis size
Dr. Pleasure	+	Patients with anhedonia

(continued)

Psychiatrist's Surname	Indication	Diagnostic Presenting Problem
Dr. Plopper	?	Encopretic patients
Dr. Ponce De Leon	?	Patients with senile dementia
Dr. Rockaway *also* Dr. Rockwell	?	Autistic patients
Dr. Rounds	? ? +	Anorectics Bulimics Patients who are medical students
Dr. Rudder	+	Patients who are directionless in life
Dr. Rumble	?	Patients who are gang members
Dr. Sadoff	− −	Suicidal patients Depressives
Dr. Sage *also* Dr. Sageman	+	All patients
Dr. Salter	−	Suicidal patients with high blood pressure
Dr. Sass *also* Dr. Sasser	?	Acting-out, oppositional, defiant adolescents
Dr. Sasseville	?	Acting-out, oppositional, defiant patients suffering from the delusion that they are "Beatniks"
Dr. Share	+	Humanistic patients
Dr. Showstack	?	Exhibitionists
Dr. Sleeper	?	Narcoleptics
Dr. Speaker *also* Dr. Speakman	+	Elective mutes

(continued)

Psychiatrist's Surname	Indication	Diagnostic Presenting Problem
Dr. Took	?	Cleptomaniacs
Dr. Twentyman	?	Patients with multiple personalities
Dr. Um	?	Inarticulate patients
Dr. Uzee	−	Learning disabled patients who do not know where "v," "w," "x," and "y" go in the alphabet
Dr. Warm	+	All patients
Dr. Wee	?	Enuretic children in therapy
Dr. Wise also Dr. Wiseman	+	All patients
Dr. Worst	−	Patients concerned with quality of medical care
Dr. Yap	+	Nonverbal patients
Dr. Zarzar	−	Stutterers

References

American Psychiatric Association. (1989). *American Psychiatric Association Biographical Directory 1989*. Washington, DC: Author.

Krankman, E. von. (1989). Therapist surname and the presenting problems of psychotherapy patients: Implications for treatment and therapy outcome. *Journal of Polymorphous Perversity, 6*(1), 16–23.

How to Be a Good Psychotherapy Patient

David A. Levy, Ph.D.

University of California at Los Angeles

THERE IS A MULTITUDE of books and articles devoted to teaching people how to become effective psychotherapists. However, there is a dearth of literature on how to become good psychotherapy patients. The purpose of this article is to offer you some practical guidelines, suggestions, and techniques that can help you make the most of your psychotherapy experience.

Conducting Yourself in the Psychotherapy Session: Twenty Easy "Dos" and "Don'ts"

By far, the most challenging (and yet potentially the most entertaining) aspect of being a psychotherapy patient concerns your relationship with your psychotherapist. It is crucial, from the opening moments of the first phone call, that you get your therapist to like you, to become dependent on you, and to become convinced that only he has the power to cure you. While your therapist is busy delving deep into the inner recesses of your psyche and of your wallet, just follow these 20 easy-to-learn techniques and in virtually no time at all you'll have him or her eating out of the palm of your hand.

1. *Do* attribute all of your successes to your therapist, and all failures to yourself.

2. *Do* gaze reverently into your therapist's eyes as he pontificates about the nature of the human condition.

15

3. *Do* occasionally confuse something that your therapist said with something that Freud said.

4. *Do* complain about insensitive and judgmental parents, teachers, and, especially, prior psychotherapists.

5. *Do* apologize profusely to your therapist for not showing faster improvement.

6. *Do* casually inform your therapist that you're due to come into large sums of money in the near future.

7. *Do,* at random moments, say to your therapist, "You *really care* about me, don't you?"

8. *Do* tell your therapist that you passed up a week in Tahiti just so you wouldn't have to miss your therapy session.

9. *Do* tell your therapist that when you win the Nobel Prize, you will announce to the world that you owe it all to him.

10. *Do* tell your therapist that you're totally committed to sticking with therapy—even if it takes 50 years.

11. *Don't* point out that your therapist constantly contradicts himself.

12. *Don't* embarrass your therapist by waking him up when he dozes off in the middle of your session.

13. *Don't* tell your therapist that his mind is obviously on everything else in the world, other than what you're saying.

14. *Don't* tell your therapist that his interpretations of your dreams are about as helpful as last year's horoscope.

15. *Don't* say to your therapist, "So, tell me something I *didn't* know."

16. *Don't* say to your therapist, "For *this,* I'm paying you money?"

17. *Don't* say to your therapist, "At least a plumber guarantees *his* work!"

18. *Don't* say to your therapist, "What's the matter? Not smart enough to get into law school?"

19. *Don't* say to your therapist, "Is doing therapy the *only way* you can get your intimacy needs met?"

20. *Don't ever* say to your therapist, "But what should I *do* about my problem?"

Secondary Gains and Fringe Benefits: Getting the Maximum Mileage from Being a Psychotherapy Patient

Irrespective of what actually happens (or doesn't happen) in the course of psychotherapy, the very fact of being a psychotherapy patient can proffer you powerful leverage in all of your interpersonal relationships. Here are four easy pointers.

1. Hide Behind Diagnostic Labels

You can deftly absolve yourself of all personal responsibility for your behavior by cloaking yourself in psychological diagnoses. For example, if someone is in any way critical of something you've done, just retort: "Hey, what do you *expect* from me? I'm a passive-dependent personality type with low-grade, uncrystallized borderline personality features!"

2. Use Therapy Against Your Mate

Having an argument with your mate? No problem! Regardless of the content of the argument, you're sure to render your opponent powerless by smugly delivering the line: "Well, at least *I'm* in therapy. What are *you* doing to help this relationship?"

3. Get Back at Your Parents

When your parents ask you why you're in therapy, you have your choice of two very powerful strategies, either of which is guaranteed to leave them speechless and riddled with feelings of guilt and self-doubt.

a. The Passive-Aggressive Maneuver

To execute this maneuver, simply follow this prescribed sequence: (1) look confused and disappointed, (2) emit a mildly exasperated, "some-people-never-learn" sigh, (3) walk away, slowly shaking your head and muttering under your breath.

b. The Direct Frontal Attack

For this tactic, just look them both straight in the eyes and shout with great vehemence, "I'll give you two guesses!"

4. Impress Your Friends

When in the company of your friends, make a habit of using psychological terms that you've picked up in your psychotherapy sessions and from watching television shows. Show them how "deep" you are by talking glibly about faulty introjects, repressed libido, inflated personas, irrational belief systems, incomplete gestalts, maladaptive learning patterns, ontological insecurity, dysfunctional family systems, your critical "inner-parent," your battered "inner-child," and your obnoxious "inner-aunt." Occasionally, squint your eyes, tilt your head, and ask people, "Don't you think you're projecting?"

A Final Word

Remember that *it's not easy* to become a good psychotherapy patient. Millions of people never learn. But, *don't get discouraged!* Trust that *you can do it!* Make these strategies a part of your life, and you're well on the way to complete recovery and true mental health.

A Phrenologist's Guide to Effective Therapeutic Intervention Within the Psychotherapy Setting: The Pipe Method

Barry A. Schreier and Heidi R. Thummel

University of Missouri at Kansas City

A case study is presented as a means of exploring the reformulation of phrenology as a modern-day therapeutic school of thought. Therapeutically produced cranial convexity is introduced as a means of changing the ineffective thought processes of select clients diagnosed as "problem individuals." Implications are drawn regarding the removal of the use of blunt instruments from the closet and their reintroduction into the therapist's office as a means of achieving therapeutic goals. A new axis for the DSM-III-R is proposed and possible contraindications for the pipe method are discussed.

SINCE THE DAWN of humankind, members of the species have used blunt instruments to change the mental processes of their fellow humans (Kubrik, 1969). This primitive manifestation of what the authors call "cranial recalibration" ultimately developed into the science of phrenology (Haddock, 1918). During the brief life of this soft science, practitioners of phrenology examined epidural hematomas in the pursuit of localizing and mapping the strengths and liabilities of various personality categories.

Phrenology was thought to have died some time ago, having been blamed for numerous fatal mishaps. However, the key concept behind its philosophy—that the use of blunt instruments applied to the cranium can bring about effective modification in human behavior—has continually resurfaced in some of the leading psychotherapeutic interventions of modern practice (the labotomizer [ice pick or spoon], electroshock electrodes, etc. [Lenol, 1954]).

The current authors feel it is time for mental health professionals to rid themselves of the constant denials and rationalizations[1] regarding blunt instrument applications within the therapeutic process, for the development of the Pipe Method is predicted to bring about a resurgence in the use of blunt instruments in changing the ineffective thought processes of clients.

This form of therapy was developed at the Seattle Orthopsychiatric Rehabilitation and Research Youngsters unit (SORRY). At SORRY, children and adolescents are seen with disorders ranging from Attention-Deficit Hyperactivity Disorder (314.01) to Zoophilia (302.90) (in other words, disorders from A–Z). Our involvement with an adolescent who had several such disorders led to the accidental discovery of the absolute effectiveness of the application of blunt instrumentation in the therapeutic process. This striking discovery will be discussed in the following case study.

The Case of Delbert P.

Incident 1

When Delbert arrived at SORRY, he was suffering from an Agreeability Deficit Disorder (000.01) that manifested itself in his inability to stop trading his lunch at school (999.98), shaving the neighbor's cat (999.97), watching reruns of the Donna Reed Show (999.96), taking double dares (999.95), spitting into the wind (999.94), eating crackers in bed (999.93), stepping on cracks and breaking his mother's back (999.92), doing his James Brown impression at the Annual Seattle Soul Festival (999.91), howling at the moon (999.90), using fluorocarbons (999.89), playing in heavy traffic (999.88), teasing the neighbor's pitbull (999.87), letting friends drive drunk (999.86), urinating in the Annual Seattle Swimming Pool Festival, which is held in direct conjunction with the Annual Soul Festival (999.85), drinking gutter water (999.84), reading Danielle Steele novels (999.83), dealing from the bottom of the deck (999.82), making left-hand turns between the hours of 4 and 6

---

[1] Since these ego defense terms (i.e., "denial" and "rationalization") have been used, the entirety of this investigation will be considered a psychoanalytic study and therefore the use of statistics need not, and will not, be used (see Freud, 1899).

(999.81), choosing Coke repeatedly in the Pepsi Challenge (999.80), and voiding where prohibited by law (999.79).

Delbert also refused to take out the trash (999.78), wash his hands before dinner (999.77), clean behind his ears (999.76), floss after each meal (999.75), change his underwear on a regular basis (999.74), use Wisk® for that annoying ring around the collar (999.73), substitute Nutra-Sweet® for those sugary snacks (999.72), pay his American Express bill in full (999.71), wear a hard hat in a hard hat area (999.70), and look for the union label (999.69).

Needless to say, Delbert was disagreeable.

Traditional psychotherapeutic techniques were found to be clearly ineffective in dealing with these unusual manifestations of a commonly diagnosed clinical disorder.

One day, while in a play therapy session of Cowboys and Indians (Wayne, 1955), Dr. X became deeply involved in the attainment of the therapeutic goal and took after Delbert with a lead pipe. After cornering Delbert, Dr. X struck him cleanly on the forehead, which immediately rendered Delbert agreeable.

To measure the extent of Delbert's agreeability, the Pepsi Challenge was administered. Delbert chose Pepsi 30 trials out of 30. This was seen as a brilliant therapeutic success for Dr. X and thus also for Delbert.

Dr. Ihava Haddock was consulted at the Institute of Phrenology. It was determined that Dr. X struck Delbert in Region 8—the Agreeability Area of the Phrenological Mapping of the Mind. It was hypothesized that Delbert's Agreeability Area was concave at birth and therefore deficient in nature. When Dr. X struck Delbert in Region 8, his once concave Agreeability Area became remarkably convex, thereby strengthening and increasing his tendency toward agreeability. To test the positive connection (a qualitative statistic) among therapeutically produced convexity in deficient brain regions, the use of cranial recalibration, and its facilitation of positive attributes, the authors decided to strike Delbert again.

Incident 2

Delbert had not only suffered from dramatic disagreeability, but also carried a secondary diagnosis of Concentration Deficit Disorder

(000.02). We contacted Delbert's teacher, Miss Landers, concerning Delbert's Concentration Deficit Disorder. Miss Landers related that Delbert always shifted his eyes toward the classroom windows (888.87) during rote memorization of histology lessons.

Once again, Delbert was clearly a problem.

We SORRY researchers decided to enlist the aid of Miss Landers in cranially recalibrating Delbert's Region 4 (Concentration Area) through therapeutically produced cranial convexity. Miss Landers' assistance was solicited because she has always been such a swell teacher (Cleaver, 1988).

As Delbert's gaze began to wander over toward the classroom windows during rote memorization of histology, Miss Landers was instructed to strike him as hard as she could in Region 4 with a lead pipe.

When Delbert engaged in the inappropriate target behavior, he was instantly and unexpectedly struck in Region 4. Immediately following this therapeutic cranial recalibration, Delbert's concentration improved remarkably, as evidenced by his glassy-eyed stare at the chalkboard throughout the remainder of that day.

Discussion

The Delbert P. case study demonstrates conclusively (a qualitative statistic) that cranial recalibration via the pipe method is a highly and permanently effective therapeutic means by which to alter defective mental processes.

The SORRY researchers feel that this bold new method, based on a bold old idea, will bring the use of blunt instrumentation as a therapeutic tool out of the closet and back into the office of modern psychotherapeutic practices.

The following contraindications are to be noted: (1) A pipe method rider will need to be attached to liability insurance policies to cover possible lead poisonings stemming from skin breakage or terminal recalibrations (Peckinpah, 1975); (2) cranial recalibration should not be attempted with anyone who has a chronic heart condition, acute lumbar difficulties, high blood pressure, or who is in the third trimester of pregnancy; and (3) cranial recalibration should only be implemented with a 5-pound lead pipe. Blunt instruments other than a lead pipe (e.g., baseball bats, hockey sticks, crow bars, or Aunt Millie's vase) have not been standardized for cranial recalibration and therefore should not be used.

It should be noted that research efforts are currently being directed toward the development of a sixth axis for the use of *DSM* diagnoses. This new axis will allow the would-be "cranial recalibrator" to easily make the proper diagnosis as to which phrenological area recalibration should be directed.

Future research might focus on those annoying situations that sometimes arise when dealing with transference issues. A possible area of further study might be the feasibility of removing the clients from the traditional clinical setting and actually taking them "out back" for cranial recalibration. The number of attempted client runaways from this natural setting could serve as an indicator of the depth of the resistance in the transference.

References

Clever, B. (1988). *Miss Landers' guide to parochial etiquette: Gee Beav, Dad's sure gonna holler.* Mayfield, USA: Golly Publishers.

Freud, S. (1899). $N=1$: *A psychoanalyst's guide to statistical significance.* Vienna: Strategrasse Bar & Grill Publishers.

Haddock, Ihava. (1918). Phrenology: Intra-cranial resectionary tactics involving cross-dissected incisional workings of the bidilusionary. *American Journal of Phrenology, 5,* 50–51.

Kubrik, S. (1969). *2001: A space odyssey.* A livingroom, Kansas City: Saw part of it.

Lenol, Ty. (1954). *Thorn in my side: A look at vestibular bleeding and the use of blunt instrumentation.* Walla Walla, WA: Alopecia Publishers.

Peckinpah, S. (1975). Chain death murder. *Journal of Slow Motion Violence, 666,* 132–456.

Wayne, J. (1955). *I'm O.K., you're not: The disassociation of the west from the Seattle Indians.* Twin Cities & Tri-Counties: Sybil Publishers.

The Effect of Computer Enhancement on Marital Longevity

Jim Weis, Ph.D.

FOR YEARS SOCIAL SCIENTISTS, the clergy, and the makers of Corning Ware all watched helplessly as the nuclear family exploded into the mushroom cloud of divorce. Various methods, from marriage counseling to open marriage, have been employed in an effort to stem the skyrocketing divorce rate in the United States, but nothing has been successful. Until now.

Finally, after all these years of frustration and heartbreak, Dr. Wilda Dorian, Professor of Computer Science at Carmichael College in Payne City, Georgia, has developed a revolutionary therapeutic technique that could turn out to be the greatest discovery in the field of domestic relations since the prenuptial agreement. This Madame Curie of family therapy calls her panacea for divorce "Computer Enhanced Marriage." Many of her colleagues are already saying that Dr. Dorian will virtually eradicate the scourge of divorce, much as Dr. Jonas Salk conquered the once-dreaded disease of polio.

Recently, in an extremely frank and candid interview with this author, Dr. Dorian confided that her interest in this area of research stemmed from her own divorce several years ago when she terminated her 20-year-old marriage because, in her words, "Quite frankly, my significant other had gotten old, dumpy, and wrinkled."

Dr. Dorian explained that if she had only known what her mate was going to look like in 20 years, she never would have married him in the first place. And thus the concept of Computer Enhanced Marriage was born. With the help of anthropologists, dentists, and plastic surgeons, Dr. Dorian developed a computer software program that is able to predict the effects of aging on 50 human features.

After rigorous cross-examination, Dr. Dorian finally confessed that she learned of this remarkable technique, not from a conference on medical technology at MIT or an article in a scientific journal, but by watching the FOX television network program, "America's Most Wanted." A Philadelphia sculptor named Frank Bender used computers to help create a bust of the murderer, John List, who had been missing for 18 years. The bust was shown on "America's Most Wanted," and shortly after, List was captured. The sculptor's rendition of the aging process proved to be uncannily accurate, right down to List's saggy jowls, hair loss, and style of eyeglasses.

Dr. Dorian concluded that if computer enhancement could help capture a wanted criminal, it might also be used to curb this country's divorce rate. Her method is simple. Some time between the engagement and the blood test, she shows her patients what their prospective mate will look like in 20 years. Her findings have been astounding.

"The single greatest cause of divorce," Dr. Dorian avers, "is the precipitous, impulsive marriage, based solely on physical attraction. Our society sends people into marriage with a false psychological orientation. As Dr. Freud wrote in *Civilization and Its Discontents,* it is 'as though we were to equip people starting on a polar expedition with summer clothing and maps of the Italian lakes.' Starry-eyed lovers sometimes need a brutal dose of reality."

At the conclusion of the interview, Dr. Dorian provided a demonstration of her revolutionary technique at the Zsa Zsa Gabor Institute for the Study of Marital Longevity. The laboratory subjects were a young couple named Troy L. and Melissa B., who held hands and looked into each other's eyes continuously. They were obviously very much in love, and they agreed to take part in Dr. Dorian's experiment only because it paid well and they were saving up to buy a washer and dryer.

Troy and Melissa were a handsome pair, and both were in top physical condition. He maintained his prepossessing form by lifting weights. She stayed in shape by engaging in jogging five times a week. When Dr. Dorian showed the couple what they would look like in 20 years, the results were shocking. Troy's stomach bulged beneath the white belt of his green plaid pants. His hair had disappeared from his head, and instead sprouted from his nose and ears. Melissa looked like Golda Meir. Her hourglass figure melted like Salvador Dali's clocks.

"I can't believe I ever gave you the time of day," Troy said in disgust.

"Feeling's mutual, Tubby," Melissa shouted, throwing her engagement ring in his face.

"One more senseless divorce nipped in the bud," Dr. Dorian sighed with a sense of deep personal satisfaction.

At this time, 10 state legislatures have introduced bills requiring Computer Enhanced Marriage, and Dr. Dorian is confident that soon her technique will be adopted worldwide. Some critics have charged that Dr. Dorian's discovery is curbing divorce only because it discourages couples from getting married, but Dr. Wilda Dorian is not concerned with this criticism.

"I agree with the English novelist, Thomas Hardy," she responds, "when he wrote 'If a way to the better be, it requires a look at the worst.' Now, if you will excuse me I have a lunch date. Come along Troy."

The interview was concluded. This author was escorted from the Gabor Institute, and the brilliant Dr. Dorian was out to lunch.

Building Patient Loyalty: The TherapyPlus™ Frequent Patient Program

A. J. Foltman, Ph.D., Psy.D.

ONE OF THE MOST SERIOUS problems we face as psychotherapists is the lack of patient loyalty to the therapy process. This often leads to "therapist shopping," lateness, missed sessions, premature termination on the part of our patients, and, most important, irritation and reduced income for the therapist. Noting the many novel business and marketing concepts adopted and adapted from fields other than psychology that have been advanced in the *Journal of Polymorphous Perversity* (see, for example, Humphreys, 1990; Lee, 1991; Spicer, 1990; von Krankman, 1990), the author investigated still other areas to see what motivational techniques might be borrowed, creatively altered, and applied to maximize therapists' incomes. The airline industry proved to offer one of the most innovative, powerful, and robust means for increasing repeat customer business—the frequent flyer program. The author presents here a natural extension of the airlines' frequent flyer program as it is applied to psychotherapy patients—the TherapyPlus™ Frequent Patient Program.

Earning Therapy Minutes

The basic unit of the TherapyPlus™ Frequent Patient Program is the TherapyPlus™ Minute. These minutes are earned at the following rates:

Type of Session	TherapyPlus™ Minutes
Enrollment Bonus	100
Full Fee, First Class Session* (50 min.)	100
Full Fee, Economy Class	50
Seven-day Advance Purchase Session**	25
SuperSaver Session, Intern Therapist	20
SuperSaver Session, Student Therapist	10
Waiting List	10 (per week)

*Includes licensed psychologist, full leather recliner or couch, upgrade tissues, complimentary beverages and dream interpretations, and concierge check-in.
**Non-refundable.

Membership Tiers

The TherapyPlus™ program recognizes different membership tiers based upon the intensity of participation of patients in the program. The Basic membership is for the majority of patients seen on a once-a-week or several-times-per-week basis.

A special TherapyPlus™ Analysand membership is available for those especially loyal and frequent patients. There are two categories of Analysand members, which are determined according to the actual therapy minutes accumulated over the previous calendar year:

Category	Actual Therapy Minutes	Bonus
Analysand Terminable	2500	50% per session
Analysand Interminable	5000	100% per session

Analysand members are also rewarded with many special benefits for their loyalty to the psychotherapy process. For example, current 1992 Analysand members receive their own membership card, special express check-in services, toll-free telephone numbers for appointment changes, and a reserved section of the waiting room suitable for the special needs of the intensive, introspective, psychoanalytic psychotherapy patient. In addition, Analysand members receive our annual newsletter, *Forever,* at no extra charge. Valued Analysand Interminable members also have exclusive, free use of special Analysand Interminable reserved parking spaces.

Award Structure

There are many exciting and valuable free awards and upgrades from which TherapyPlus™ members can choose in exchange for their therapy minutes. Note that there are both Premium and SuperSaver awards.

TherapyPlus™ Free Awards

	TherapyPlus™ Minutes	
Award	Premium	SuperSaver*
Free Telephone Consultation (15 min.)	500	250
Free SuperSaver Session	1000	500
Free Economy Session	2000	1000
Free First Class Session	4000	2000

*SuperSaver awards not available Christmas, Hanukkah, New Year's Day, Easter, Passover, May 6 (Freud's birthday), or after 4:00 PM weekdays and all day Wednesdays and weekends.

Upgrade awards are also available. The Upgrade Award structure follows.

TherapyPlus™ Upgrade Awards*

Award	TherapyPlus™ Minutes
Upgrade to Current Issues of Magazines in Waiting Room	100
Upgrade from Generic to Name-Brand Tissue	200
Upgrade to Intern Therapist from Student	200
Upgrade to Licensed Psychologist from Intern	1000
Upgrade to Individual Therapy from Group Therapy	1000
Upgrade to Family Therapy from Marital Therapy	1000
Upgrade to Full Leather Recliner or Couch	2000

*Per session. May not be combined with other awards.

Special Incentive Bonuses

From time to time the TherapyPlus™ Frequent Patient Program offers special incentive bonuses, such as 100 TherapyPlus™ minutes for each referred patient who actually enters therapy.

Concluding Remarks

Psychotherapy providers will likely find that the TherapyPlus™ Frequent Patient Program is both exciting and lucrative. The author feels that the program is the best in the industry and that it will effectively cut down on the inconveniences associated with patients' lack of commitment while ensuring increased income for the psychotherapy practitioner. Of course, the TherapyPlus™ program has required some minor adjustment and restructuring of service delivery, but the results have been gratifying in terms of greater patient loyalty. The author already has seen several patients self-refer (as well as lay claim to 100 TherapyPlus™ minutes for having referred patients—themselves—who actually entered therapy) after having read brochures describing the TherapyPlus™ Frequent Patient Program distributed in major airports. The author anticipates many, many more.

References

Humphreys, K. (1990). Franchising unorthodox, eclectic psychotherapeutic services: Psychotherapists-R-Us. *Journal of Polymorphous Perversity, 7*(2), 3–4.

Lee, S. D. (1991). Advances in the marketing of psychological services and products. *Journal of Polymorphous Perversity, 8*(1), 7–8.

Spicer, J. (1990). Marketing strategies for the counseling professional: Ideas that make dollars and sense. *Journal of Polymorphous Perversity, 7*(2), 16–18.

von Krankman, E. (1990). Contingencies of reinforcement in pizza parlors and psychoanalysis: Toward an application of the principles of reward in overcoming resistance to psychoanalytic treatment. *Journal of Polymorphous Perversity, 7*(2), 16–18.

A Twelve-Step Program for the Dead

Terrel L. Templeman, Ph.D.

Oregon Trail of Technology

The *Journal of Polymorphous Perversity* was the first publication to address an often neglected though certainly grave topic in the field of psychotherapy, namely therapy of the dead (Menahem, 1984; Templeman, 1984). Although published studies employing psychotherapy and pharmacotherapy demonstrated promise in clinical trials with dead clients, mental health professionals have generally found this type of client most resistant to entering treatment (Burke & Hare, 1988). Recently, a self-help literature for the dead has been promoted as an alternative to therapist-directed approaches (Barnum, 1989), but the low sales of books such as *Dead Who Love Too Much* and *Dead No More* suggest that the dead are not receptive to this approach either.

My colleagues and I at the Oregon Trail of Technology believe that a new approach to this lifeless field must be undertaken if the dead are to be engaged in treatment effectively. We present here for the first time a 12-step program for the dead, which is modeled closely after other 12-step programs. Dead Ones Anonymous (DOA) groups allow the dead to meet in supportive, anonymous settings to develop mutual trust and to realize that they are not alone in their dead pursuits. Most dead come from dysfunctional families, and we have encouraged DOA members to share their feelings about the burden of being unjustly maligned or irrationally revered by the living, a burden strikingly apparent in the facial expressions of group members. Topics in these groups range from ego boundary problems (especially salient for the borderline dead) to living up the expectations of others. (We have discovered that living up to anything can be very difficult for the dead.)

Unlike other 12-step programs, DOA groups are best facilitated by a non-dead member. Without at least one living participant, these meetings often degenerate into protracted and embarrassing silences. The facilitator also helps to keep participants focused on the 12 steps, not to mention sitting upright in their chairs.

What Are the 12 Steps?

1. Accept the fact that you are dead. Stop fighting it. Remind yourself that death is simply nature's way of telling you to slow down.

2. Take responsibility for your own inertia. Stop blaming it on those around you. Remember, today is the first day of the rest of your death.

3. Give your burdens up to a higher power and don't try to play God. Recite the Serenity Prayer and pray for the wisdom to know the difference between life and death.

4. Take a holiday. In fact, take a vacation once in a while. Don't take death so seriously. Remember, you only die once.

5. Remind yourself that death is a disease. It begins the day you are born, progresses until the day you die, and then takes over completely. For 10 out of every 10 people, this disease is fatal.

6. Admit that you are powerless over death. If you thought life was unmanageable, just try keeping all your loose ends together when you are dead!

7. Make a searching and fearless mortal inventory of yourself. See what you can find.

8. Humbly ask someone to see that your grave is kept clean.

9. Know that you are not alone in this affliction.

10. Remember that things could always be worse.

11. Relinquish materialism and let go of worldly possessions. Remember, you can't take it with you.

12. Strive for a spiritual awakening as long as you are dead, and remember: It's never too late to try for heaven.

The Role of the Family

Family members are encouraged to attend other groups for survivors, codependents of the dead, and adult children of the dead. These groups allow family members to better understand their own dysfunctional relationships with the dead, usually rooted in an inability to bury the past. Toward this end, family members are taught an intervention called the Interment, which helps them to lay to rest not only unresolved conflicts with the dead but the body of the problem itself. Families are generally greatly relieved after the Interment, although for the dead themselves it is only the first step to recovery. Thus, therapists in our program are encouraged to work individually with the dead after the Interment, as much uncovering is necessary before dead clients are ready to attend group meetings.

References

Barnum, Jr., P. T. (1989). Waking the dead: New markets for old ideas. *Bibliotherapy Today, 12,* 1–25.

Burke, E., & Hare, W. (1988). Engaging the recently dead for science and profit. *Necrotherapy: Theory, Research, and Practice, 104,* 312–320.

Menahem, S. E. (1984). Psychotherapy of the dead. *Journal of Polymorphous Perversity, 1*(1), 3–6.

Templeman, T. L. (1984). [Letter to the editor]. *Journal of Polymorphous Perversity, 1*(2), 3.

Short-Term Cognitive Therapy for Authors of Rejected Manuscripts

Ernie Ness, Ph.D., and Elson Bihm, Ph.D.

University of Central Arkansas

WRITING FOR PUBLICATION is not an easy task. Even after putting untold hours of blood, sweat, and tears into a manuscript, there is no assurance that it will be accepted. Rejection rates run as high as 97% in some journals (for example—the *Journal of Polymorphous Perversity* [G. C. Ellenbogen, personal communication, March 22, 1991]).

Anyone who has been in the publication game for long knows all too well the intensity of feelings that goes along with rejection (Ness, 1986). But finally, help is available. For authors who have been rejected and who now must live with the accompanying pain and anguish (Bihm, 1987; Bihm & Ness, 1987), we have a solution. Beneath all—and we mean every single one—of the unpleasant emotions that rejection may foster are readily identified cognitions (Ness & Bihm, 1988).

In this article we share 14 irrational beliefs that underlie publishing anxiety, depression, and despair. We have gleaned these fundamental beliefs from several years of doing therapy with "rejects," that is, authors of rejected manuscripts. Following each belief we have provided a more rational response that is of unquestionable value to the discouraged masses who have received those heartless "Dear Rejected Author" letters. The responses were taken directly either from transcripts of therapy sessions or from notes we made after consoling one another.

I must publish.

There you go "*must*erbating" again. How many times do we have to tell you to stop doing that?! You would prefer, like, or even want to publish. Besides, what's the worst that could happen if you don't publish? Tenure, promotions, and providing for your family aren't everything in life. There will still be beautiful sunsets, children at play, the smell of fresh hay, and 122 new journals a year that might need your manuscript.

I must have the approval of the editorial board.

These are people you don't even know. Why should you care about them? If it is acceptance you want, look somewhere else. And remember, two people from the same board reading your work may have two entirely different reactions. Now *that* is irrational and makes no sense to us either. So really, you need only the approval of the majority of the editorial board. Find out where they live and send them gifts.

There is no future for me.

Now doggone it, there you go catastrophizing. In fact, there is a future for you. It just may not be in academia. There is life after rejection. Einstein, Edison, and others too numerous to mention suffered many defeats but didn't give up; of course, they were only doing civilization-altering work and not trying to get published in an esoteric journal. Never mind.

I am a miserable failure.

Leave the adjective out of there. There is no empirical basis available by which to measure degree of failure. Besides, this is a classic example of overgeneralization. You're probably highly successful at something. Think about it. Think about it a long time if you have to.

The acceptance of manuscripts is capricious and unfair.

Put the sour grapes away. Nobody said life was fair. We all know that a manuscript rejected by one journal may well get published in another. Try putting someone else's name on your cover page and see what happens. Use a name like Beck, Cattell, or Lazarus.

There is one, and only one, journal for which my work is appropriate.

Balderdash. Only a narcissist would utter a statement as foolish as this one. Maybe your field of study is a little narrow; try expanding it. Consider a vanity journal; it might cost a few hundred dollars for reprints but at least you're published. And remember, being published in a prestigious journal isn't everything; others will just come to expect more and greater things of you. Now there's some pressure you don't need.

My best work will go unread by future generations.

Not to insult you or anything, but isn't that the fate of nearly everything that is published these days? So your article on "A Linguistic Analysis of the Word 'Abnegate'" goes unseen. If you're that hung up about it, start your own journal. Or, place your work in a time capsule, bury it, and leave instructions for your children's children to open it later. If you simply cannot wait, then follow Martin Luther's example: nail your manuscript to the front door of a public building.

It's the end of the world.

Talk about a gross exaggeration. The world, as most of us know, will end according to the scripture when we least expect it . . . (sometime early in June, 1996). Get back to the business of writing.

I have been personally rejected.

No, you have been professionally rejected. Oh sure, the pain lasts for a very long time but you will recover. If you believe in blind reviews, then you know the reviewers had no idea who you were. Unless one of them lifted their blindfold, just for a moment, to sneak a peek.

Trash gets published but my manuscript is rejected.

You can lament this all you want but it doesn't change a thing. Wait, now that you mention it, it really is kind of amazing the kind of work that gets published these days. Of course, some journals aren't too particular and will take almost anything—provided it's on a familiar topic, uses some incredibly complex statistical procedure, or has an author with a name like Beck, Cattell, or Lazarus.

I can't stop now. I've put too much time into this.

This is clearly a personal choice; you can stop but you will not. This manuscript must have some special meaning for you. Let go of it. When you talk like this you sound like someone with a very serious addiction. Perhaps our group for Adult Authors of Rejected Manuscripts would be useful.

This was my best effort. I'll never be able to write again.

Nobody likes a quitter. And frankly, learned helplessness does not become you at all. Seek inspiration. Go see "Field of Dreams." Continue to refute defeatist thinking. Think a wonderful thought, any little thing will do.

I'm going to hurt the members of the editorial board.

Whoa! Hold that thought. We have an ethical obligation to meet here. Revengeful thoughts are commonplace. But please don't act on them. Rage will get you nothing but a jail term and, almost surely, will delay publication. And, as long as you're at it, give any weapons you own to a trusted friend—preferably one who has been published.

If I don't publish, I will perish.

Fruit perishes, people die. And you won't die. You might wander into the existential void for a spell if you get yet another rejection, but it could be worse. To prove our point, take out that rejected manuscript again and read the negative, cruel, and painful remarks one more time. There. Put it down. We said *put it down!*

Conclusion

There you have it—our prescription for the cognitive treatment of rejected authors. Our success rate has been remarkably high. Well, actually we cannot locate any data to support that statement, but we do know that one session is sufficient for most clients because very few return for a second.

Our next paper will focus on personality characteristics of the rejected author. We suspect there is a gene that predisposes some writers to become depressed, angry, and homicidal upon being rejected. And it's a good bet that the environment exerts some kind of influence.

References

Bihm, E. (1987). *It hurts so bad: Rejection*. Unpublished manuscript.
Bihm, E., & Ness, E. (1987). *Unpleasant feelings following rejection: A factor analytic approach to understanding*. Unpublished manuscript.
Ness, E. (1986). *Ouch! Rejected again*. Unpublished manuscript.
Ness, E., & Bihm, E. (1988). Rejection: You can only take so much of it before you are just ready to explode. *Journal of Last Resort, 23* (1), 216–223.

2

Psychoanalysis

Contingencies of Reinforcement in Pizza Parlors and Psychoanalysis: Toward an Application of the Principles of Reward in Overcoming Resistance to Psychoanalytic Treatment

Ernst von Krankman, Ph.D.

IN BOTH THE PIZZA PARLOR and psychoanalysis businesses, the business owners have been traditionally faced with the problem of motivating the clientele to return. This is a dilemma particularly as both businesses pretty much depend on repeat customers. Wily pizza parlor managers, intrinsically pragmatic in nature, have had no hesitation in applying the scientifically based principles of the behavioral sciences in attempting to modify customer behavior to fulfill their own needs—profitability and nice cash flow. However, the same cannot be said for psychoanalysts who, reluctant to employ the principles of modern day learning and motivational theory, suffer lower clientele return rates (also known as "higher drop-out rates") than do pizza parlor owners. Viennese-like vendors of psychoanalysis could learn a lot about enticing their customers to return by looking to their Neapolitan business brethren for key motivational paradigms.

For these merchants of mozzarella cheese, tomato paste, and dough only one key motivational principle has been effective in ensuring consistent sales of pizza pies—put the customer on a reinforcement schedule for reward. In theory, nice and clean; in practice, simple and easy to implement: For each pizza pie ordered the customer gets credit toward a *free* pizza pie. Earn enough credits, and the free pizza pie is yours. (See Figure 1.) It is not hard to imagine how a similar reinforcement schedule could be implemented for the customers of psychoanalysts. (See Figure 2.)

Armed with a scientifically based motivational tool borrowed from pizza purveyors, psychoanalysts will now be able to counteract the powerful forces of "resistance" that so often undermine the course of psychoanalytic treatment—and lead to premature termination of the all-important psychoanalyst-customer relationship.

Sal's Pizzeria & Trattoria

314 E. 3rd Street (Corner 1st Avenue)
New York City
626-2642 (or M-A-M-A   M-I-A)
"The finest in Italian cuisine since 1973."

Have your host clip this coupon upon purchase of any whole pizza. You get a free plain pizza (extra toppings 50¢ each additional) after 10 pizzas.

Your Hosts: Sal & Maria Tortellini

# OF PIZZA PIES PURCHASED										
1	2	3	4	5	6	7	8	9	10

Figure 1. Sample of a pizza parlor coupon employed to motivate customers to return.

Quality Interpretations Since 1936   *Most Insurance Plans Accepted*

SEYMOUR FRUITLOOPER, M.D., PH.D.
PSYCHOANALYST

262 Central Park West   Telephone: (212) 227-3228
Suite 1-A   or
New York, New York 10024   (212) A•B•R•E•A•C•T

Patient is "entitled" to one (1) free 50-minute session of psychoanalysis upon completion of 10 years (5-days-a-week) treatment. Loss of this card will be interpreted as a passive-aggressive act and no replacement card will be issued.

YEARS OF PSYCHOANALYSIS										
I	II	III	IV	V	VI	VII	VIII	IX	X

Figure 2. Sample of a psychoanalysis coupon employed to motivate customers to return.

Crazy for Loving You: Notes From Week One of the Psychiatrists' Strike

James Gorman

MONDAY: Came in today needing to talk. I was very antsy. I had that pressured speech you hear from schizophrenics. Not that I'm schizy. Sure, I'm on medication. I'm a pharmacological construct like everyone else. But it's nothing heavy—an anti-depressant, a little lithium, sometimes a tad of something from the benzodiazepine family to take the edge off. So who do I find filling in for Stanley because of the strike? Enid, the agoraphobe. Only now she doesn't mind leaving home like this because not only the shrinks but the doormen and the elevator operators are on strike. Enid is also afraid of elevators and doormen.

I lie down on the couch and I tell her my dream. It has to do with this enormous tree, something like a redwood, and a guy in a dark hat with a beard, kind of Chassidic-looking, carrying an axe. I didn't actually have this dream, but I want to test her on something easy before I give her real material. She does pretty well. She knows that Stanley is Jewish, as was Freud, and she quickly pegs the guy with the axe as a mohel, which of course explains the tree.

What really surprises me is that she actually seems concerned about me—not something I ever noticed in Stanley. This, after all, is a woman who understands fear. Castration, wide-open spaces, elevators—what's the difference? We are discussing ways to bolster our courage—real support-group stuff, not the sort of thing Stanley charges a hundred and seventy-five dollars an hour for—when my time runs out. I suggest she skip her next patient so we can have a cup of coffee together. She agrees. Since she is not in fact a shrink, we figure there is no ethical conflict.

TUESDAY: Jack, the depressive, is Shrink-for-a-Day. Jack is the patient Enid cancelled yesterday. He is wearing a dark three-piece suit and pointy-toed wing tips. He has a pad in his lap, and he is grinding his teeth while he sharpens a pencil with a small custom-made penknife.

Immediately I start to have associations that I am not willing to disclose to a layman. I have only met Jack once, when all Stanley's patients got together to figure out a schedule during the strike, and I'm sure you can imagine the things I'm thinking. A depressed guy, with a pathetic stub of a pencil, whittling it down even smaller? With analysts like this, who needs dreams?

I must say, however, that Jack does the silence very well. In my experience this is one of the tough moves for shrinks. Stanley was all right at the silence, he could hold on for quite a long time, but you could hear him breathing and shifting around and fidgeting. That always reassured me. I can't hear a thing from Jack. It comes to me with some force that I am lying down, in a very vulnerable position, and that behind me, where I can't see him, is a mental patient with a knife. Am I crazy?

Finally Jack breaks the silence.

"What's the thought, Ted?" Boy, you can tell one of Stanley's protégés a mile away. What's the thought, indeed.

"I was just wondering what you do, Jack—you know, regularly?"

"I'm a doorman."

"Oh."

WEDNESDAY: My day. Jack turns out to be not such a bad guy after all—some fairly sticky psychosexual conflicts, and not a lot of ego strength, but not a bad sort. The standard approach with a patient like this is to support the defenses, not to probe too far too fast. I notice that Jack is still sharpening the pencil—it's down to paper-clip size, just about—but I don't challenge him on it. We talk about superficial issues mostly—how the doormen's strike threatens his sense of self, and how betrayed he feels that just when he needs Stanley most Stanley abandoned him. I point out that Stanley may feel the same way about his doorman.

None of the other patients are much of a challenge either: Ellen is a copy editor at an electrical engineering journal. Her presenting problem is difficulty concentrating on her work. My diagnosis: absence of castration anxiety. Thomas is on the rebound from a therapist who freed his inner child, thus causing him to move all his capital from biotechnology to toys, just before the Gulf War. Now he hopes to make a killing on his Schwarzkopf action figure. Obviously Oedipal. Gary, who has questions about his sexual identity, clearly suffers from a full-blown narcissistic personality disorder. He takes all strikes personally. Striking screenwriters are depriving him of movies. When the sanitation men went out it was because they hated his garbage. Gary has been through quite a number of psychiatrists and is convinced that his dreams alone have caused them to walk. With Enid, I decide to attack her agoraphobia with something unconventional: I take her to an Imax film about the Grand Canyon. Breakthrough! Afterward we go to her apartment for tea and Tylenol.

It is Florence who causes me the most difficulty. She enters the office slowly, looking straight at me with a smoky gaze. My first impression is of a young woman in black net stockings, with psychosexual conflicts. I cannot help noticing her full red lips (wet look) and firm and shapely breasts. Indeed, Florence is in therapy because she acts out sexually and has poor impulse control. Countertransference sets in immediately. I know, of course, that if I, as her analyst, fall prey to her charms, as so many other men have, rather than remaining concerned and helpful at a distance, I will be doing her no good. On the other hand, I'm not actually her analyst.

THURSDAY: Off day. I meet Enid at her place. She says she is not coming out anymore, ever again. Apparently she has found out about me and Florence, whom she refers to as a decompensating tramp. I point out that (a) although Florence may have some sexual issues to work through, she is not a tramp; (b) as a friend of mine, and nothing more than that yet, Enid has no business diagnosing my other acquaintances; (c) as a sometime analyst of mine she has no business making value judgments and directive comments about my sex life; (d) as my patient it's none of her business.

FRIDAY: Florence's day. Enid stays home. Jack, encountered at the end of his hour, looks happier than usual. For me countertransference and transference have become inextricably entangled. I ask Florence if the same sort of thing goes on with all her patients.

"What's the thought?" she says.

I am beginning to suffer from confusion. Wednesday I was a shrink. Last night I was a doorman. Tomorrow I'm a porter. People I hardly know ask me if I live in my own building. Every day I have a different analyst. They all seem to think I suffer from hidden sexual conflicts.

On my way out, I see Stanley in the elevator, operating it. The encounter is awkward for both of us. I thank him for letting us continue to use his office during the strike, and I compliment him on how close the elevator and the lobby floor line up when he stops. I can see him formulating a question, some probe, some pipe-munching aperçu, and then stopping himself, abruptly, as if this would violate the passenger-operator relationship. It's a sad moment.

"Watch your step," he says.

"Thanks," I say. "See you next week."

3

Psychodiagnostics

On the Differential Diagnosis and Treatment of an Uncommon Clinical Syndrome: The Normal Personality Disorder

Melanie E. Harrington, Kriss Kline, and Niloofar Afari

University of Nevada at Reno

THE PSYCHOPATHOLOGY OF NORMALCY is one of the least researched topics in psychology. Indeed, the assumption underlying most courses in psychopathology is that such behavior is somehow "abnormal" (e.g., see the titles of textbooks by Davison & Neale, 1989; Sarason & Sarason, 1989). Needless to say, these textbooks scarcely mention Normal Personality Disorder (NPD). This is particularly troublesome in view of the insidious and chronic nature of NPD. The present paper reviews what little does exist on NPD and provides suggestions for assessment and treatment of the disorder.

Diagnostic Concerns

The essential feature of NPD is a pervasive and chronic pattern of severe normalcy that affects virtually every aspect of the patient's existence. Patients may exhibit a gross inability to experience excessive anxiety, obsessive thoughts, or delusional ideation. These people are typically incapable of real commitment, as evidenced by their need for "vacations," "reexamining one's life plan," and "going with the flow" (Felix, 1972). It goes without saying that NPD is not typically encountered among graduate students.

A peculiar aspect of NPD patients is their ability to exhibit intense fear when confronted by fear-provoking stimuli without this conditioning being generalized to other situations. In fact, NPDs are usually *inca-*

51

pable of so-called "neurotic anxiety": this exacerbates their characteristic inability to sustain brief, clinging relationships; to attain high achievement goals (e.g., doctorate degrees in psychology); and to enjoy Woody Allen movies.

Associated Features. Interestingly, empirical work suggests that NPD is rarely confounded by other syndromes (Insurance Companies of America, 1922). However, recent case studies have revealed pathological aspects of the NPD's behavior that were previously unnoticed: this suggests that additional diagnoses should be carefully considered on a case by case basis (Third-Party Payment Recipients, 1923).

An acute syndrome is sometimes noted that mimics this disorder. Patients with severe NPD may appear Normal for a limited period but the symptoms will quickly escalate under stress-inspired conditions. Occasionally, substance use, sleep disturbance (e.g., during class), or apathy ("Hey, pal, I've already got tenure") may mask this disorder.

Impairment. It is ironic that NPD patients may initially seem to be functioning quite adequately. It is not unusual for patients to remain in therapy for months, even years, before accompanying impairments are uncovered.

Predisposing Factors. A familial pattern of sub-clinical normalcy is often present. For example, NPD parents are more than five times as likely to produce NPD offspring as are abnormal control parents (see review of low-risk studies by Boring, 1987). Results of twin and adoption studies have been unable to identify any specific genetic component to the disorder; however, we're pretty sure there probably is one. Specific environmental stressors appear to detract from, rather than add to, the risk for NPD.

Prevalence and Sex Ratio. Prevalence estimates vary wildly, from a low of 0.0% (Psychiatric Billing Service, 1988) to a high of 100% (Szasz, 1978). These equivocal results can most likely be explained by the methods used to calculate NPD prevalence rates. The formula for prevalence of NPD, as derived by Lumper and Splitter (1980), is as follows:

$$N - (\sum X_a...X_z) = n(NPD)$$

where N = all the people in the world, X_a = number of people who answered the Minnesota Multiphasic Personality Inventory (MMPI) as if they had disorder A, X_b = number of people who answered the MMPI as if they had disorder B, (and so on), and $n(NPD)$ = number of people who answered the MMPI without demonstrating disorder A to Z in some response or another.

In the past, NPD has often been described as a predominately male disorder (by males). However, current popular literature suggests that females are equally at high risk.

Proposed Diagnostic Criteria

As in the *DSM-III-R*, the present authors have taken the view that virtually all aspects of human living are subject to diagnosis. Nonetheless, it is difficult to identify specific criteria for NPD because of the ambiguous and counterintuitive nature of the syndrome: it is usually the *lack* of symptomatology that is initially most apparent. Following is the proposed diagnostic criteria that the authors have gleaned from the empirical literature on the topic.

Diagnostic Criteria

NPD patients present with a pervasive and chronic pattern of severe normalcy. Onset usually follows puberty, but it is not infrequent for the disorder to extend throughout the lifespan. The disorder must affect several areas of functioning; *all* of the following are characteristic.

1. Excessively and painfully appropriate in social interactions

2. Shows marked inability to engage in disordered thought

3. Oriented x 3 (Note: this symptom may be absent under conditions of Volitional Pharmacological Intervention [VPI])

4. Lack of physiological deviation, including but not limited to nor-

matensive, regular heartbeat, remarkably unremarkable EEG, uninterpretable EMG

5. Patient does not meet criteria for *any* disorder listed in the *DSM-III-R* (quite a remarkable achievement in and of itself)

Treatment Considerations

It should be noted that chronic NPD types have a very poor prognosis: they are typically not motivated to seek therapy and, in fact, may exhibit opposition to therapeutic intervention. Psychoanalysis is the preferred method of treatment for these patients as it is very difficult to focus on specific problems and this particular patient population usually thinks behavior therapy is silly, anyway.

Assessment Considerations

The following responses are typically found when employing a variety of psychodiagnostic instruments.

1. MMPI profile:

	T-Score	H Y				M A					T-Score
	110	P				S		P	S		110
	100	O	D		P	C		S	C		100
HIGH	90	C	E	H	S	U	P	Y	H	H	90
	80	H	P	Y	Y	L	A	C	I	Y	80
	70	O	R	S	C	I	R	H	Z	P	70
AVERAGE	60	N	E	T	H	N	A	A	O	O	60
	•—•—•—•—•—•—•—•—•										
	50	D	S	E	O	I	N	S	P	M	50
	40	R	S	R	P	T	O	T	H	A	40
LOW	30	I	I	I	A	Y	I	H	R	N	30
	20	A	O	A	T	/	A	E	E	I	20
	10	S	N		H	F		N	N	A	10
		I				E		I	I		
		S				M		A	A		

2. Rorschach: Card V (held upright): "It looks like a bat." (Sometimes also includes, "No, really, I don't see anything else.")

3. Beck Depression Inventory: Score of zero ("I haven't been think-

ing about killing myself much lately," "My thoughts aren't bizarre and inappropriate," "I'm not so depressed that I can't crawl out of bed," "Everybody in the world loves me," etc.)

Conclusions

Given that obscure clinical syndromes are of the most interest to clinicians, it is surprising that NPD has not been the subject of more in-depth research. Clearly, NPD patients are as capable of paying their bills as their more apparently pathological counterparts. Why, then, has the disorder received so little attention? Perhaps the answer lies, in part, in the inability of clinical psychologists to empathize with NPD patients, as the psychologists themselves are unlikely to have ever experienced similar symptoms. Perhaps what is needed, then, are more Normal psychologists who, themselves suffering from the syndrome, are better able to relate to these patients, to conduct research that represents a more empathic perspective, and to create effective approaches to working with this dysfunctionally functional population.

References

Boring, I. M. (1987). *Subjects at low risk for attention from psychologists: The uninteresting antecedents of normalcy.* Manuscript rejected by *The Journal of Normal Psychology.*

Davison, G. C., & Neale, J. M. (1989). *Abnormal psychology* (5th ed.). New York, NY: Wiley.

Felix, O. C. (1972). Dirt and vacations: A nice combination for the obsessive-compulsive traveler. *Journal of Housecleaning and Psychopathology, 4,* 218–219.

Insurance Companies of America (Supported by Big Government). (1922). Psychologists and their dirty hands on our money: Not if we can help it. *Journal of Insuring Witchcraft and Astrology, Special Issue: Is Clinical Psychology a Science?*

Lumper, I., & Splitter, U. (1980). Calculating incidence of psychopathology: It depends on who you work for. In I. B. Scammin (Ed.), *Using statistics to find yourself.* Las Vegas, NV: Roll of the Dice Press.

Psychiatric Billing Service. (1988). *Everybody must get stoned: Why all of you meet diagnostic criteria and we don't.* Payupsville, NY: Handed Down From God Press.

Sarason, I. G., & Sarason, B. R. (1989). *Abnormal psychology* (6th ed.). Englewood Cliffs, NJ: Prentice-Hall.

Szasz, T. (1978). *The myth of mental illness, or who believes in biology anyway?* Dualist City, MA: So Sue Me Press.

Third-Party Payment Recipients. (1923). Witchcraft and astrology: The evidence in favor of granting these disciplines third-party payments. *Psychology Today,* the serious part, p. 11.

On the Fractionated Personality Disorder

Morton S. Rapp, M.D.

Whitby Psychiatric Hospital
Whitby, Ontario, Canada

THE MULTIPLE PERSONALITY DISORDER (MPD), a malady in which "The essential feature . . . is the existence within the person of two or more distinct personalities or personality states" (American Psychiatric Association, 1987, p. 269), has gained much popularity in usage among members of the clinical community. This relatively new diagnostic entity has only been in vogue during the second half of the 20th century. It remained rare until the 1950s, when scientific advances in the area were bolstered by two critical discoveries: (1) there's a sucker born every minute, and (2) books describing MPD ultimately were highly lucrative for their authors.

Controversy has certainly always surrounded the MPD diagnosis. Its supporters claim that many patients who were subjected to severe child abuse early in their lives tend to evidence MPD later on, and further, that those who would challenge the validity of this may themselves suffer from MPD. Its detractors maintain that the features describing the disorder can be better fit into already existing diagnostic categories and that there is little reason to create a new, and perhaps misleading, diagnosis such as MPD. The present author feels that this diagnosis has heuristic value and presents here a related and ancillary disorder—the Fractionated Personality Disorder (FPD).

Rationale

In mathematics every number has a reciprocal. For example, the reciprocal of 2 is $\frac{1}{2}$. It follows logically that if individuals exist who have more than one personality, then there must be others with only a fraction of a personality.

Empirical Base

No studies have been performed to test the hypothesis of the FPD. It was felt that the intrusion of coarse methods such as standardized interviews, or the intervention of psychiatric epidemiologists, would cheapen the area of study—and possibly ruin the author's chances of success in launching his forthcoming book(s) on this exciting new diagnostic entity.

Etiology

The specter of child abuse probably underlies much of the FPD, as illustrated in the following case.

MR, a 16-year-old teenager of Yuppie background, had been enjoying a successful career as a malingerer until his 16th birthday. On that date, his father refused to buy him a Jaguar Sovereign, stating that the family's second car (a 5.0 liter Mustang) would have to do. The patient's father had a history of child abuse, having previously forced MR to study and to refrain from using LSD. MR, upon hearing that the Jaguar was "no-go," immediately stopped speaking English and become a $\frac{1}{3}$ personality," characterized by sleeping 16 hours a day. A cure has yet to be devised for this case.

Clinical Features

Despite a lack of systematic study, workers in the field of FPD have identified a number of characteristic epidemiological features of FPD.

1. It may occur in males, females, and those who have not yet decided.

2. It is more common in right-handed people.

3. In Japan it is more common in Orientals, whereas in Central Africa it is found more frequently among blacks.

4. The age range is from 0 days to 98.5 years.

5. It is surprisingly common among people who are in need of a clinical diagnosis to excuse some otherwise inexcusable behavior.

6. It is more common among certain occupational groups, e.g., accountants, librarians, and psychiatric hospital administrators. It is conspicuously absent from one occupational group—lawyers— suggesting that these professionals may have no personality whatsoever.

Quantitative Ecology

The diagnosis of FPD lends itself to easy quantification. For example:

$$P(FPD) = N + B(\text{Power } L/D) \times 1/R$$

where P(FPD) is the probability of a clinical case suffering from a FPD, N is the number of current believers among Ph.D. candidates and medical interns, B represents the number of financially successful books on the topic to date, L is the lurid nature of the FPD patient's history measured in standard luridity units, D reflects the number of detractors of the diagnostic entity with measured IQs of 90 or greater, and R is the square root of the FPD-related books to be found in the remaindered section of the main Barnes & Noble Bookstore on lower Fifth Avenue in Manhattan.

Future Directions

Much research is called for in assessing the reliability and validity of the Fractionated Personality Disorder. One fruitful avenue for investigation might be determining the smallest fraction of a personality to be found in a single individual. For example, from a clinician's perspective, a $\frac{1}{8}$th personality would be all that much more interesting to work with than would a $\frac{1}{2}$ personality. Although there are (as yet) no data to support the existence of an Exponential Personality (where the personality would be represented mathematically by 2 to the nth degree), or possibly even a Square Root Personality, this may merely reflect the fact that our present research tools are still too crude to discern the presence of such personality entities.

Conclusions

The author has described the presence of a diagnostic entity that supplements the Multiple Personality Disorder—the Fractionated Personality Disorder. The manuscripts for six books on this elusive diagnostic disorder have already been completed and copyrighted by the author. A new, major motion picture loosely based on one of these volumes is slated for release in a movie theater near you early next summer. Diane Keaton will star.

References

American Psychiatric Association. (1987). *Diagnostic and statistical manual of mental disorders* (3rd ed. *revised*). Washington, DC: Author.

"Life to Go"[1]: The Relationship of Country Music to Psychopathology

James M. Stedman, Ph.D.

University of Texas Health Science Center at San Antonio

Victor S. Alpher, Ph.D.

University of Texas Health Science Center at Houston

"I'M GONNA LIVE FAST, love hard, die young, and leave a beautiful memory." . . . "Jack Daniels, if you please, knock me to my knees." . . . "My wife ran off with my best friend and I miss him."

What do these Country Music lyrics have to tell us about the human psyche and the everyday stuff of human order and disorder? Certainly, early efforts to capitalize on the interface between Country and Western (C & W) and social science were made by Pennebaker et al. (1970) in their penetrating study of social perceptions. These researchers, no doubt sons and daughters of the pioneers, electrified the social psychology field by demonstrating a hypothesis generated within country music by Mickey Gilley, namely that "All the girls get prettier at closing time." Not only did these investigators demonstrate this significant truth empirically, but they also challenged all social scientists and mental health practitioners to explore the depths of country music, a veritable gold mine of testable hypotheses regarding human, and sometimes animal, social relationships.

---

[1] Jackson, Stonewall (ca 1957). Life to Go. Written by George Jones, Columbia: BMI.

The authors wish to apologize in advance for sexist language found in this article. Regrettably, country songwriters have not yet adopted a non-sexist language policy.

Though well within the spirit of Pennebaker et al.'s challenge, this article is not an empirical study. Rather, it attempts the first step of any scientific inquiry—classification. In a word, we set out to sort out the psychopathological and therapeutic insights of country music. Our database was "The List," a compilation of country lyrics first collected in an unsystematic fashion by Walt Garrison and other members of the Dallas Cowboys organization. There is little doubt that these pithy but penetrating phrases and sentences go straight to the heart of much of psychopathology, particularly as conceptualized from traditional viewpoints.

Much of the descriptive psychopathology of human relationships is covered within C & W and this has been true since Country emerged from the backwoods of the Southeastern states in 1927. From the time of that first recording session on a hot, muggy July day in Bristol, Virginia, troubled souls from Jimmy "The Singing Brakeman" Rogers and the late and great Hank Williams, Sr., to Dolly "9 to 5" Parton, have moaned the blues of marital strife, alcoholism, identity crises, guilt, major depression, and such. Few recall exactly what those first hillbillies twanged out but, no doubt, it had to do with major pathology. Among the earliest recordings listed in the 1925–28 Columbia catalogues were such titles as "Little Rosewood Casket" and "Boston Burglar," no doubt early references to modern-day concepts of complicated bereavement and antisocial personality.

The reader will find that the following lyrics depict various diagnostic categories and, in general, cover most that is real in human misery. Though short in the areas of schizophrenia, bipolar disturbance, and drug abuse (cuz true kickers may drink but they don't put harmful chemicals in their bodies, a few notable "Outlaws" excepted), C & W does cover the full range of alcohol abuse, depression, neurosis, personality disorders, and adjustment problems.

1. Depression

Several categories of depression and coping with environmental stress seem represented, so we have broken them into categories.

a. Existential

"I don't know whether to shoot myself or go bowling."
"Liars 1, Believers 0."
"Drop kick me, Jesus, thru the goal posts of life."

b. General

"If today was a fish, I'd throw it back."
"I'm sick and tired of wakin' up so sick and tired."
"I'm too low to get high."
"Them that ain't got can't lose."
"A sad song don't care whose heart it breaks."

c. Relationship Related

"Don't cry down my back, baby, you might rust my spurs."
"I only miss you on days that end in Y."
"If you're ever in Houston, look me down."
"Pick me up on your way down."
"Please put her out of my misery."

d. Alcohol Related

"I'm going to put a bar in my car and drive myself to drink."
"When the hangover's over, your memory's still hangin' on."

2. Relationship / Marital / Family Pathology

Much of C & W leaves the exact nature of the relationship pathology ambiguous. However, much is specific to marriage.

a. General Relationship Issues

"I wouldn't take you to a dog fight even if I thought you could win."
"She stepped on my heart and stomped that sucker flat."
"She went to the bathroom and never came back."
"Flushed from the bathroom of your heart."

"When the phone don't ring, you'll know it's me."
"You must think my bed's a bus stop the way you come and go."
"He 'little thing'ed her out of my arms."
"Just because you got to first base don't mean you're home free."
"It was always easy to find an unhappy woman until I started looking
   for mine."
"Third rate romance, low rent rendezvous."

b. Specific to Marriage / Divorce

"Our marriage was a failure but our divorce ain't working either."
"My wife ran off with my best friend and I miss him."
"She got the gold mine and I got the shaft."
"If you want to keep the beer real cold, put it next to my ex-wife's
   heart."
"I gave her a ring and she gave me the finger."
"I gave up Good Morning Darling and We Love You Daddy for
   this."
"A woman a day keeps my man away."
"It ain't love but it ain't bad."
"For better or for worse but not for long."
"Does my ring hurt your finger when you go out at night."
"I'm afraid to come home without warning."

c. Family

"If I get stoned and sing all night long, it's just a family tradition."

3. Alcoholism (a well-represented category)

a. General

"The alcohol of fame."
"I'd rather have a bottle in front of me than a frontal
   lobotomy."
"How can whiskey six years old whip a man that's 32?"
"It's commode-huggin' time in the valley."
"Jack Daniels, if you please, knock me to my knees."
"I'm whiskey bent and hell bound."

"I'm going to hire a wino to decorate our home . . . so
you won't have to roam."
"Four on the floor and a fifth under the seat."

b. Alcohol and Relationship

"She ain't much to see, but she looks good to me thru the bottom of
a glass."
"When the hangover's over, your memory's still hangin' on."

4. Personality Disorders

This diagnosis is well represented but skewed toward antisocial and
borderline states.

a. General

"It's bad when you're caught with the goods."
"On the muscle of my arm there's a red and blue tattoo saying, "Fort
Worth, I love you.""
"Up against the wall, Redneck Mother."
"I'm gonna live fast, love hard, die young, and leave a beautiful
memory."
"I turned 21 in prison, doing life without parole."
"Lyin' here, lyin' in bed."
"I turned out to be the only hell my mama ever raised."
"You can't make a heel toe the mark."
"Tell ol' 'I ain't here' he better get on home."
"Ol' Glen lived himself to death."

b. Relationship Related

"I'm going to the dogs with a bunch of swinging cats."
"Walk out backwards so I'll think you're coming in."
"From the gutter to you is not up."
"She caught me lying and then she caught a train."

c. Borderline States

"I've always been crazy but it's kept me from going insane."
"I don't know what it is but I sure miss it when it's gone."
"When I'm alone, I'm in bad company."
"It's not love but it's not bad."
"It's morning and I still love you."
"She'll love you to pieces but she won't put you together again."
"She feels like a new man tonight."

5. Miscellaneous

There are a scattering of other pathologies represented.

a. Sadomasochism

"It seems the best in you brings out the worst in me."
"You went out of your way to walk on me."

b. Identity Disorder

"I'm going some place I hope I find."
"There's no use running if you're on the wrong road."
"You pretend I'm him and I'll pretend you're her."

c. Narcissistic Personality Disorder

"Oh Lord, it's hard to be humble when you're as perfect as me."
"What's mine is mine and what's yours is mine and that's the way
  it's always been."

d. Defense Mechanisms—Denial / Repression / Selective Attention / Projection

"I've closed my eyes to the cold hard truth I'm seeing."
"She took everything but the blame."

e. Superego Conflict—Guilt

"Somewhere between lust and sitting home watching TV."
"I'm ashamed to be here but not ashamed enough to leave."

f. Paranoid States

"If you keep checking up on me, I'm checking out on you."

g. Sexual Potency

"If you can fake it, I might make it."
"It takes me all night long to do what I used to do all night long."

Well, those are our classifications and, heck, we know they ain't perfect. There are overlap problems, e.g., alcohol sloshing over into depression and starcrossed relationships, but, hey, that's real life. And, as noted, C & W is very light on commentary about the obsessive-compulsive and other "nice," higher functioning neurotics, the sort all therapists crave as patients but are so hard to find these days. Also, there's not much about schizophrenia, organic stuff, or mania in there either.

So, what about therapy applications? No classification article would be worth it's salt or lime without some comment on treatment applications, and we offer a few examples of how the sophisticated therapist might put Country to use.

1. Applied to divorced parents continuing to undercut each other for the kid's love—"You know, Brad and Jan, 'Your Marriage Wasn't Great But This Divorce Ain't Workin' Either.'" Of course, the therapist must paraphrase a bit, but you get the picture.

2. For counseling with an alcoholic—"Joe, it sounds like you're headed for 'The Alcohol of Fame'" or as an interpretation to a deteriorating alcoholic—"Clyde, you seem to be saying 'I'd Rather Have a Bottle in Front of Me Than a Frontal Lobotomy.'"

3. In family therapy with a teenage conduct disorder, whose sibs have also hit the skids at age 16—"Nick, it sounds like 'When

You Get Stoned and Sing All Night Long, It's Just a Family Tradition.'"

4. For use with the borderline patient who is just moving into another relationship—"Linda, it sounds like 'You Don't Know What It Is But You Sure Miss It When It's Gone.'"

5. As a confrontation to the hysteric—"Look, Bambi, 'You've Closed Your Eyes to the Cold Hard Truth You're Seeing.'"

6. To the antisocial good ol' boy (this confrontive clarification will be used mostly in the South and Southwest)—"Bubba, You're 'Up Against the Wall, Redneck Mother.'"

7. And, finally, for the existential therapist who might have treated Sartre—"Gee, Jean Paul, it seems that 'You Don't Know Whether to Kill Yourself or Go Bowling.'"

To sum it all up, when David Allen Coe admonished his songwriting friend, Steve Goodman, that the perfect country song had to include elements of "mama, trains, getting drunk, pickup trucks, and prison," he should have added the need to delve into schizophrenia, drug abuse, bipolar disorder, and the "nice" neuroses. On second thought, perhaps Coe realized that these subjects were already within the exclusive domain of rock music.

References

Carr, P. (1980). *The illustrated history of country music.* Nashville: Country Music Press / Doubleday.

Coe, D. (1974). You never even call me by my name. In *Once upon a rhyme,* Columbia: BMI.

Gilley, M. (1975). Don't the girls all get prettier at closing time. In *The best of Mickey Gilley, Vol. 2,* Columbia. Singleton Music Co.: BMI.

Malone, B. C. (1968). *Country Music U.S.A.* Austin: University of Texas Press.

Pennebaker, J. W., Dyer, M. A., Caulkins, R. S., Litowitz, D. L., Ackerman, P. L., Anderson, D. B., & McGraw, K. M. (1970).

Don't the girls get prettier at closing time: A country and western application to psychology. *Personality and Social Psychology, 5,* 122–125.

Sons, L. (1977). I don't know whether to kill myself or go bowling. *D (Dallas) Magazine,* pp. 122–132.

4

Psychological
Testing

Rorschach Assessment of the "Non-Living": Hardly a Dead Subject

Edward C. Budd, Ph.D.

THE DEAD HAVE LONG RECEIVED insufficient attention from mental health professionals. A literature review reveals no psychologists or psychiatrists who specialize in dead patients, no organizations of professionals treating the dead, and prohibition of third-party reimbursements for services to dead individuals. The latter is a vexing (and possibly illegal) restriction currently under investigation (Reeves, 1986). The lack of a lively advocacy group for dead consumers is problematic.

The moribund status of this field persists despite evidence that the dead constitute a fast-growing segment of the population. Elway (1987) investigated the familiarity of the public with various clinical phenomena. The percentages of respondents reporting personal knowledge of individuals in various diagnostic categories were as follows: alcoholics, 53%; mentally retarded persons, 33%; transvestites, .02%; dead people, 98%. The current number of dead Americans exceeds that at any time in our nation's history (Mecklenberg, 1985). Death has figured prominently in the lives and careers of many noted personalities such as Elizabeth Kübler-Ross (who is fascinated by death), Ronald Reagan (who seems dead), and Shirley MacClaine (who used to be dead). The great figures in the history of psychology—men like Carl Jung, Alfred Adler, and Sigmund Freud himself—actually *are* dead. In brief, epidemiological and sociological investigations justify increased focus on the dead.

Fortunately, our field's morbid aversion to investigation of the dead (or those with "problems in non-living," a phrase preferred by professionals disturbed by the pejorative connotations of the term) is lessening. Menahem (1984) published a seminal article exploring psychotherapeutic techniques with dead patients. Goldman (1987) con-

73

ducted a landmark investigation of psychological test data drawn from dead patients.

The present study addresses the lack of rigorous research regarding projective testing of the dead. Specifically, this study utilized empirically derived Rorschach interpretive hypotheses to evaluate dead patients.

Method

Subjects

Subjects were drawn from the emergency room of a public hospital. Relatives of each dead person to enter this area were asked to authorize participation of their loved one in the study. It should be noted that "dead rights" are often ignored. The fact that some individuals cannot stand up for themselves does not give license to disregard their value as persons. The first 20 dead individuals whose participation was authorized constituted the "dead" group. (Note: The author regrettably acknowledges the possibility of some sampling bias, since the next-of-kin refused permission on 197 occasions. Many of these individuals seemed particularly insensitive to the cause of science.) Twenty non-dead adults were chosen at the same site to constitute a control group.

Procedure

Initial discrimination of the dead from non-dead was accomplished on an intuitive basis. The Budd Morbidity Inventory (BMI) (Budd, 1986) was subsequently administered to all subjects, and the BMI classification was compared with initial group assignment. Interestingly, informal classification was generally accurate, with only three "false negatives." Three subjects initially classified as non-dead (two medical residents and a hospital administrator) proved to be dead on administration of the BMI. They were excluded from the study and replaced by three additional subjects to form the non-dead group. (Note: The term "pre-dead" is preferred over "non-dead" by some investigators. This usage has not achieved widespread acceptance, perhaps because of the lack of adequate longitudinal research.)

The Rorschach was administered to the 20 dead and 20 non-dead subjects by experienced clinicians. Exner's administration and scoring procedures were utilized for all subjects (Exner, 1986). Exner's 1986 text may be consulted for scoring criteria and definition of all structural variables. The author assumes responsibility for all interpretive hypotheses.

Results and Discussion

Dead and non-dead subjects were found to differ on many variables. For the reader's convenience, the most informative differences have been grouped and depicted in Table 1.

The first cluster, "Oversimplification," reflects investment of cognitive effort in the projective task. These variables represent the degree to which the subject attempts to "make sense of" his stimulus field. (Note: Masculine pronouns have been used exclusively, but the question of sexist language usage regarding dead persons is a perplexing one. The issue of "dead gender" is unresolved, and it is unclear whether he, she, he or she, he and/or she, or "it" is the correct usage.) All means for the dead subjects equaled zero, suggesting a passive disinterest in one's surroundings. The dead subjects appear to have withdrawn from the richly interwoven processes of assimilation and accommodation so vital to human adaptation. This finding dovetails nicely with the oft-cited observation that the dead seem oddly underinvolved with their surroundings.

The second cluster, "Lack of Felt Needs for Interpersonal Closeness," addresses interpersonal withdrawal on the part of the dead. The data show clearly that non-dead subjects actively experience such need states and manifest an interest in people. Conversely, the Rorschach records of dead subjects are almost devoid of such indicators. Case reports (cf. Menahem, 1984) indeed suggest that a lack of interpersonal responsiveness is an attribute of dead patients that may impede traditional forms of intervention.

The third cluster, "Richness of Internal Experience," was defined in order to encapsulate findings on a number of traditional variables. In brief, dead subjects utilized very few response determinants and restricted their responses to a minimal number of content categories. One may tentatively suggest that the internal life of the dead is characterized by a rather bleak sameness and emptiness.

TABLE 1. Rorschach Scores for Dead and Non-Dead Subjects

Variable Cluster	Dead		Non-Dead	
	Mean	SD	Mean	SD
Oversimplification				
ZF	0.0	0.0	13.2	4.1
DQ+	0.0	0.0	8.1	2.1
Blends	0.0	0.0	6.1	2.0
M	0.0	0.0	3.9	1.8
Lack of Felt Needs for Interpersonal Closeness				
T	0.0	0.0	1.1	.8
FM	0.0	0.0	3.2	1.8
H	0.0	0.0	3.6	1.7
M	0.0	0.0	3.9	1.8
Richness of Internal Experience				
Total Determinants	0.0	0.0	7.2	2.1
Total Contents	0.0	0.0	8.1	3.0
Low Rate of Behavior				
Total Rejections	10.0	0.0	0.0	0.0
Cognitive Rigidity				
WSUM6	0.0	0.0	6.8	1.4

(Note: $p < .005$ for all group differences by Blickstein's alpha test [Blickstein, 1982])

The fourth variable, total number of responses (R), is illustrative of the respondents' (or, in the case of our dead subjects, non-respondents') typical response style in an ambiguous, unfamiliar context. For the purposes of this study, it is more profitable to think in terms of "rejections"—that is, the number of cards to which the subject *refused* to offer at least one response. Non-dead subjects averaged 0.0 (out of a maximum possible of 10.0) rejections per protocol, while dead subjects provided an average of 10.0. High frequency of rejections has been associated with depression, defensiveness, or limited cognitive ability. Other aspects of dead subjects' protocols appear to rule out depression; for example, our dead subjects achieved a mean score of 0 on the Exner depression index. It is interesting in this context that dead subjects achieved a mean score of 4 on the Exner suicide constellation, supporting the observation that such individuals often seem preoccupied with morbid themes—cf. Goldman (1987). Cognitive limitations cannot be ruled out in the current study. In fact, previous research (Goldman, 1987) has suggested that cognitive impairment may be a cardinal feature of death. It also seems plausible that "defensiveness" in some sense is a major component of the psychology of deadness. Whatever the underlying psychology, our data clearly indicate that a generally low rate of behavior—at least in unfamiliar, ambiguous situations—is an important characteristic of the dead.

The final variable, the weighted sum of six special scores (WSUM6), has been included in Table 1 under the heading "Cognitive Rigidity." High scores on this variable are associated with thought disorders, suggesting an intriguing absence of schizotypal qualities among the dead. Further investigation of the biochemistry of deadness might conceivably provide a key to the treatment of schizophrenia. However, the very low mean WSUM6 of our dead subjects appears to reflect rigorous adherence to standard modes of thinking. This rigid perfectionism, or inability to "loosen up," is striking in view of the uncanny frequency of the adjective "stiff" in informal characterizations of dead persons. Note that creative works have most commonly been accomplished by non-dead individuals. In fact, it is striking that the productivity of creative individuals has almost without exception occurred prior to death.

Thus, Rorschach findings highlight the importance of five major features of the psychology of dead persons:

1. a tendency toward cognitive underinvestment in the environment;

2. lack of motivation to engage in interpersonal interactions;

3. impoverished internal experience;

4. low rate of behavior;

5. cognitive rigidity.

These findings are impressive in their "goodness of fit" with intuitive impressions of the dead. One can easily recognize in this description many factors that make interactions with the dead so frustrating. Moreover, these data suggest a possible model (albeit a speculative one) for understanding the psychology of the dead. Specifically, *death may represent an effort to adapt to problematic circumstances.* All the factors cited above are common when individuals are confronted with debilitating stressors that overwhelm other coping strategies. Thus, death may be an end-state homeostasis following the failure of numerous adaptation efforts. The "dead" form of adaptation, viewed in this way, is a uniquely successful (though costly) mode of adaptation, which eliminates or moderates discomfort when other means of adaptation have been exhausted. In the words of the author's father (Budd, 1977), "Death is nature's way of telling you to slow down." Seen in this light, death— with its associated features of chronicity and relative intractability— may be regarded as a personality disorder. Alternatively, from a learning perspective, death may be an operant non-response akin to learned helplessness. "Learned deadness" is a possible descriptor.

Systematic investigation of this hypothesis remains a task for the future. However, a brief biographical data sheet, completed by each subject (or subject's next-of-kin), provided some supporting evidence. One-hundred percent of our dead subjects had suffered a major trauma shortly before data collection (2 cases of acute illness, 3 cases of traumatic accident, and 15 cases of chronic, life-threatening illness). Such events might certainly overwhelm the coping mechanisms of most individuals. Only 10% of non-dead subjects had experienced such traumatic incidents. This finding suggests an important direction for future research.

Directions for Future Investigation

Our findings suggest a clear need for further investigation into the psychology of the dead. Specifically, work is needed regarding:

1. Conceptualization of death. Literature to date has not clarified such fundamental questions as whether death is best regarded as a clinical syndrome, a character style, a life circumstance (or perhaps a non-life circumstance), or a psychosomatic phenomenon. Terminology is equally muddled: the adoption of "necrology" is recommended in reference to the study of this topic.

2. Formalized study of the precursors of deadness. Identification of a premorbid personality type is a particularly interesting area.

3. Better definitions of death. Many studies to date have failed to document the criteria for inclusion in the dead subject pool.

4. Greater activism in the area of "dead rights" (confusion with "last rites" is regrettable but understandable). As was previously mentioned, necrology is unlikely to acquire a life of its own until the prejudicial treatment of the dead by medical insurers is resolved. Further, the absence of a consumer advocacy movement for dead citizens is problematic. Perhaps only the advent of a "Ralph Nader of the dead" will rectify this shameful situation. In the political arena, lobbying efforts on behalf of the dead are virtually nonexistent. Only during the reign of Chicago's (ironically late) Mayor Richard Daley, when dead persons comprised a formidable voting bloc, did the dead receive their political due. It is the author's hope that the present study will serve as one modest step toward acknowledgment of the importance of the dead.

References

Blickstein, A. C. (1982). Statistical analyses for studies so poorly planned that nothing else can be done. *Journal of Picky Statistical Squabbles, 1032* (4), 178–214.

Budd, A. F. (1977). Personal communication.

Budd, E. C. (1986). The Budd Morbidity Inventory: Will the real dead people please stand up. *Compendium of Irrelevancies, 76* (7), 36–41.

Elway, J. (1987). Everyman's experience of psychopathology: The bus station surveys. *Acta Esoterica Americana, 42* (1), 13–15.

Exner, J. E., Jr. (1986). *The Rorschach: A comprehensive system. Volume 1: Basic foundations (2nd edition).* New York: John Wiley & Sons.

Goldman, J. J. (1987). On the robustness of psychological test instrumentation: Psychological evaluation of the dead. *Journal of Polymorphous Perversity, 4* (1), 5–11.

Mecklenberg, K. (1985). Who's hot and who's not—the dead. *People, 12* (13), 56–59.

Menahem, S. E. (1984). Psychotherapy of the dead. *Journal of Polymorphous Perversity, 1* (1), 3–6.

Reeves, D. (1986). The dead: The true silent majority. *Journal of Mediocre Research and So-So Ideas, 101* (5), 121–129.

A Paper and Pencil Approach to Integrity Screening in the Post-Polygraph Era

Robin Kirk, Ph.D.

PROHIBITION OF THE USE of polygraph examination to determine the integrity of prospective and current employees has created a unique opportunity for professional psychologists to fill the service void left by the demise of this unreliable, invalid, but nevertheless profitable technology. This paper describes the methodology used to develop a paper and pencil measure of employee integrity and presents the final commercial version of that instrument.

The Global Objectification of Nasty Internal Factors (GONIF) test was developed in a 3 day period following final congressional action on polygraph testing. Advertising and printing deadlines precluded the use of conventional psychometric development techniques, and the author and other members of the GONIF investment group were forced to rely on a novel methodology for the construction and validation of the GONIF test. Our methodology, termed "Quick and Dirty" (Q&D), is similar in many respects to the techniques used to develop preliminary data in support of research grant applications.

The Q&D item pool development consisted of the author using his years of experience to construct 20 statements which probed subtle nuances of moral choice. The initial pool was carefully evaluated for grammatical integrity and accurate spelling. The corrected item pool was then cast into 10 forced-choice pairs based on the author's conceptual analysis of the underlying factor structure, and then it was sent for final printing.

Q&D validation of GONIF used a variation of the techniques employed by psychohistorians. Two comparison groups were chosen as representatives of the extremes of a morality continuum, and the author and two members of the investment group (all of whom were, minimally, regular readers of *Psychology Today*) answered the GONIF test as, in our best clinical judgment, the comparison group member would have answered it. A majority voting technique used in cases of disagreement resulted in a final interrater reliability coefficient of 1.0. (A full listing of the composition of the comparison group is not possible in this brief report, but one extreme included all senior members of the staffs of Presidents Nixon and Reagan; the other included Mother Teresa, Jesus, and Jane Fonda.)

Visual inspection of the comparison group scores indicated that differences seemed to be in the predicted direction, and re-voting on several tests strengthened this trend.

Full details on the validity study of GONIF are proprietary, as are the details of scoring and interpreting the instrument. Because of the limited validity data available at this time, commercial users of GONIF are cautioned to use the test only for screening, selection, promotion, termination, and prosecution decisions.

GONIF is presented in full below, and may be reproduced in scholarly research. Commercial use of GONIF is expressly prohibited for all but GONIF franchisees.[1]

GONIF Test

Instructions. This test has been designed to let us select the best possible candidates for positions with our firm. It was designed by professional psychologists with a keen sense of personal economics and very little regard for nit-picking issues of professional ethics, personal privacy, and basic fair-play. These psychologists work for us, not for you.

The test consists of a series of paired statements. Read each pair of statements and pick the one that best applies to you. Indicate your response on the attached answer sheet. You should answer honestly. You should not just pick responses that you think make you look good.

Some of the statements may seem strange, or even bizarre. Some

---

[1] Franchise information is available from GONIF Investment Group, P.O. Box 80386, Clarksville, TN 37040.

questions elicit information about the most personal and private aspects of your life, and you may be uncomfortable answering them since the results of this test are not confidential. We don't care. If you want a shot at being on our team, you have to pick one statement from each pair.

This test is timed. You have 2 minutes to complete it. Get to work.

1. I frequently have fantasies about sex with a wombat.
   My idea of a good time is throwing Gideon Bibles into the motel pool.

2. I have never been able to steal anything more valuable than a Chevrolet.
   The media would like you to think that drugs are a lot more dangerous than they really are.

3. I don't know why everybody is so upset about child sexual abuse.
   Differences of opinion are best settled by physical violence.

4. I would gladly sell secret company information for the right price.
   For the right price, I would gladly sell secret company information.

5. Most of the orgies I attend include at least 10 people.
   People are poor only if they are too stupid to steal.

6. All my responses to this test are deliberate lies.
   I plan to spend most of my time on the job sleeping.

7. I would enjoy the job of operating the euthanasia machine at the pound.
   I personally know that AIDS is not nearly as contagious as people think.

8. Toxic waste dumping would be a cost-effective way to hold down third world population growth.
   Cocaine improves concentration on the job.

9. "Ethics" is to "Business" as "Intelligence" is to "Military."
   I would not kill somebody unless I got paid at least $50 to do it.

10. The best way to get money is to steal it from somebody else.
    I think that pimps have pretty close to an ideal job.

THANK YOU FOR YOUR INTEREST IN OUR FIRM. HAVE A
NICE DAY. WE'LL BE IN TOUCH.

5

Clinical
Case
Studies

My Life: A Series of Privately Funded Performance-Art Pieces

Susan Orlean

1. Birth

As the piece opens, another performance artist, "Mom" (an affiliate of my private funding source) waits onstage, consuming tuna-noodle casseroles. Eventually, she leaves the initial performance site—a single-family Cape Cod decorated with amoeboid sofas, Herman Miller coconut chairs, boomerang-print linoleum, and semi-shag carpeting—for a second site, a hospital. There she is joined by a sterile-clad self-realized figure of authority ("Sidney Jaffe, M.D.") who commands her to "push," and then externalizes through language and gesture his desire to return to the back nine. This tableau makes allusion to the deadening, depersonalizing, postwar "good life." "Mom" continues "pushing," and at last I enter—nude. I do this in a manner that confronts yet at the same time steers clear of all obscenity statutes.

2. Coming Home Extremely Late Because I Was Making Snow Angels and Forgot to Stop

Again, an ensemble piece. But unlike "Birth," which explores the universal codes of pleasure and vulnerability, "Coming Home Extremely Late" is a manifesto about rage—not mine but that of the protonuclear family. The cast includes "Mom," "David," "Debra," "Fluffy," and my private funding source. In "Coming Home," I become Object, rather than Subject.

The piece is also a metaperformance; the more sophisticated members of the audience will realize that I am "coming home extremely late" because of *another* performance: "Snow Angels," an earlier, gestural work in which, clothed in cherry-red Michelin Man-style snowsuit, I lower myself into a snowbank and wave my arms up and down, leaving a winged-creature-like impression upon the frozen palimpsest. Owing to my methodology, I am better at it than anyone on the block. Note the megatextual references to Heaven, Superior Being-as-girl-child, snow-as-inviolable-purity, and time-as-irrelevancy. "Coming Home Extremely Late" concludes with a choral declaration from the entire cast (except for my private funding source, who has returned to reading the sports section), titled "You Are Grounded For a Month, Young Lady."

3. I Go Through a Gangly Period

A sustained dramatic piece, lasting three to five years, depending on how extensively the performer pursues the orthodontia theme. Besides me, the cast includes the entire student population of Byron Junior High School, Shaker Heights, Ohio—especially the boys. In the course of "Gangly Period," I grow large in some ways, small in others, and, ironically, they are all the wrong ways. I receive weird haircuts. Through "crabby" behavior (mostly directed at my private funding source), my noncontextual stage image projects the unspeakable fear that I am not "popular." In a surreal trope midway through the performance, I vocalize to a small section of the cast ("Ellen Fisher," "Sally Webb," and "Heather Siegel") my lack of knowledge about simple sexual practices.

Throughout the piece, much commentary about time: how long it is, why certain things seem to take forever, why I have to be the absolutely last girl in the entire seventh grade to get Courrèges boots.

4. Finding Myself

This piece is a burlesque—a comic four-year-long high art/low art exploration. As "Finding Myself" opens, I am on-site—a paradigmatic bourgeois college campus. After performing the symbiotic ritual of "meeting my roommates" and dialoguing about whether boyfriends can stay overnight in our room, I reject the outmoded, parasitic escape route of majoring in English, and instead dare to enroll in a class called "Low Energy Living," in which I reject the outmoded, parasitic escape route of reading the class material and instead build a miniature solar-powered seawater-desalinization plant. I then confront Amerika's greedy soullessness by enrolling in a class called "Future Worlds," walking around in a space suit of my own design, doing a discursive/nonlinear monologue on Buckminster Fuller and futurism.

Toward the end of "Finding Myself," I skip all my "classes"—spatially as well as temporally—and move into an alternative environment to examine my "issues." At this point, my private funding source actually appears in the piece and, in a witty cameo, threatens to withdraw my grant. Much implosive controversy. To close the performance, I sit on an avocado-green beanbag chair and simulate "applying to graduate school."

5. I Get Married and Shortly Thereafter Take a Pounding in the Real-Estate Market

A bifurcated work. First, another performance artist, "Peter," dialogues with me about the explicit, symbolic, and functional presentations of human synchronism. We then plan and execute a suburban country-club wedding (again, with assistance from my private funding source). Making a conceptual critique of materialism, I "register" for Royal Copenhagen china, Baccarat crystal, and Kirk Stieff sterling. Syllabic chants, fragments of unintelligible words like the screeches of caged wild birds gone mad—this megatonality erupts when I confront my private funding source about seating certain little-liked relatives. At the work's interactive climax, "Peter" and I explode the audience/performer dialectic and invite the audience to join as we "perform the ceremony."

The second part of the piece—a six-month-long open-ended manifesto on the specificity of place—culminates with "Peter" and me purchasing a four-and-a-half-room coöperative apartment with a good address in Manhattan. Conran's furniture, Krups appliances, task-specific gadgets (apple corers, pasta makers, shrimp deveiners), and other symbol-laden icons are arranged on-site. Curtain goes down on the performers facing each other on a sofa, holding a *Times* real-estate section between them, doing a performative discourse lamenting that they have "purchased the apartment at the peak of the market."

The series will continue pending refinancing.

6

Neuropsychology

The Self-Adjusting Neuropsychological Report

Colin D. Field, M.Sc.

Institute for Iatrogenic Intervention
Adelaide, Australia

BUSY NEUROPSYCHOLOGISTS often find themselves without the time to write comprehensive, punchy, readable reports these days, even when they do understand the concepts involved. In response to this sad state of affairs, the Institute for Iatrogenic Intervention has recently developed a ready-to-use, self-adjusting neuropsychological generator.

One of the Institute's best innovations, this report writer should cut out hours of toil, pen-biting, wear and tear on elbows, staring out of windows, or having to stay home from the golf course—naturally, aspiring young neuropsychologists are always at risk of suffering from these unfortunate circumstances.

Manual Version

Instructions. Simply strike out the words that do not apply.

Dear (Doctor / Lawyer / Magistrate):

Re: (Mr. / Mrs. / Miss / Ms. / Prof. / Rev. / Dr.) Smith

Thank you for referring (Mr. / Mrs. / Miss / Ms. / Prof. / Rev. / Dr.) Smith for neuropsychological assessment. May I congratulate you for selecting the top neuropsychologist in the (room / city / state / country / southern hemisphere / northern hemisphere / universe) to provide this report. You will receive an account for services in due course.

I found (Mr. / Mrs. / Miss / Ms. / Prof. / Rev. / Dr.) Smith to be a (pleasant / unpleasant) (man / woman / gent / lady / child / fellow) who appeared on first glance to be (well / depressed / dead / alive / secretly amused / secretly amusing / on all fours).

(He / She / It) was given a (wide / narrow / complete / incomplete) range of neuropsychological tests and proved to be quite (stupid / intelligent / all right / maze-bright / maze-dull).

(His / Her / Its)(Verbal / Performance)IQappearedtobe(higher / lower) than expected given (his / her / its) premorbid intelligence estimate, raising the possibility that (he / she / it) is (demented / depressed / absent / cheating / disinterested).

(His / Her / Its)(lackofinsight / lackofeyesight / lackofglasses / lack of understanding / lack of English) might have adversely affected the results.

(His / Her / Its) memory was (good / bad / big / small / memorable / forgotten), particularly following (interference / an hour / his departure / her departure / its departure / my departure).

(His / Her / Its) visuospatial abilities were (good / bad / ugly / square / variable / static) but this could be explicable in terms of (his / her / its) (death / absence / blindness / financial insolvency).

(His / Her / Its) frontal function was (frontal / stunning / stunned) as (he / she / it) could not (sort / draw / think of / pick out) more than (0 / 7 / 49 / 643) (words / numbers / concepts / red triangles) within the 2 (second / minute / hour / lifetime / dollar) time limit. In addition, (he / she / it) suffered from a characteristic inability to adopt the (abstract / flexible / reasonable / horizontal) attitude.

Overall   (Mr. / Mrs. / Miss / Ms. / Prof. / Rev. / Dr.)   Smith (passed / failed) (his / her / its) neuropsychological test session and may be considered (above / close to / alongside / well below) average compared to others of (his / her / its) (age group / socioeconomic group / education level / hat size), and appears to be (suffering from / enjoying) a (mild / moderate / severe) degree of (brain damage / back pain).

I would like you to return (him / her / it) to me next (week / fortnight / month / payday / tax time / year) for follow-up assessment, but don't even bother to make another appointment until you pay the account for this one.

Yours faithfully,

[Your name here]
Clinical Neuropsychologist

Computer Version

Interested readers should note that a computer-generated version of this generator is also available (Field, 1987, 1988). Using this version provides the added advantages that the computer will also randomly choose words from the available alternatives, will randomly select a billing amount of between $538.83 and $978.55, will automatically print a "pay immediately" account in addition to the report itself, and will, if necessary, also randomly generate patient names for bulk billing purposes. All of this will of course "cut out the middle man" completely, and will enable the young neuropsychologist to hasten to the golf course without concern for trivial details such as patient contact.

References

Field, C. D. (1987). *The computer in clinical neuropsychology: It's my parity and I'll cry if I want to.* Adelaide, Australia: Ova-Byte, Inc.

Field, C. D. (1988). *The self-adjusting neuropsychological report writer* [Computer program]. Adelaide, Australia: Ova-Byte, Inc.

7

Educational
Psychology
and
Education

Scholarly Image Enhancement
Through a Meaningless Publication

Steven J. Gilbert, Ph.D.

State University of New York at Oneonta

THE PURPOSE OF THIS PAPER is to enhance my perceived scholarly qualifications by padding my vita and reprint packet with an additional, but entirely bogus, published article (Booth, Mather, & Fuller, 1982). A variety of devices are used to make the paper look like a credible effort, rather than a crass exercise in self-aggrandizement (Freud, 1908; Jackson, Schwab, & Schuler, 1986; Schaller, 1986). For example, the first two sentences of this paragraph contain references. With the exception of the Freud (1908) citation, these references were chosen at random from the bibliography page of a recent introductory psychology text (Baron, 1989), and have nothing to do with the topic of the paper. I hope, however, that the casual reader will take the string of references to mean that I did an extensive database search, and that this paragraph represents a thoughtful and thorough review of the literature. Actually, there is a theory that explains how this would happen (Petty & Cacioppo, 1985), but it won't be explicated here, because no one who is reading this paper really cares.[1]

Some readers may question whether the *Journal of Polymorphous Perversity* has sufficient prestige to fulfill the author's self-promotional

---

[1] The Freud (1908) reference is included because a Freud reference always looks good, especially to a nonpsychologist on a committee that might be reviewing my file. I make this point in a footnote, rather than in the body of the text, because footnotes suggest that the author has penetrated some phenomenon more deeply than is reasonable to expect an ordinary reader to follow. This makes me look smart, and dedicated to precision and completeness—admirable qualities in any candidate.

99

goals. Probably not. It is hoped, however, that the same careless skimming that would enable phony references and a stupid footnote to impress a peruser of my reprints would apply to the name of the journal as well. For example, a reader might assume that the journal is a serious publication dealing with varieties of sexual dysfunction. Some might misread the name as the *Journal of Polyfaceted Perceptivity,* the *Journal of Polysocial Prehension,* or even *Scientific American* (if I luck out). Such assimilation into conventional schemas is a well established phenomenon (Allport & Postman, 1945; Bartlett, 1932; Piaget & Inhelder, 1969), but I won't go into it, because it is too late for a little psychology to transform this enterprise into a real journal article.

And therein lies the danger. A few judges of my credentials actually may recognize that this paper is not a serious piece of psychological work. What, then, will they take it to be? I'm in the most trouble if the content of the paper is accepted at face value; only an amoral creep would attempt to fool his colleagues into thinking he wrote more real papers than he did. Preferably, the paper would be accepted as satire; the author would be understood as wishing to imply that many of the papers that appear in professional journals (and thus, in curriculum vitae) are no more significant than a paper about nothing, or a paper about itself (Wittgenstein, 1958).

The question, then, is whether the author should include the document currently before the reader as an entry in the former's vita (and should the passive voice be eschewed in further sentences)? Would inclusion of the article devalue the rest of the author's publications, most of which are perfect exemplars of precisely the kind of work the present paper lampoons (assuming the present paper is, indeed, satire)? Can anyone, including the author, know for sure what this paper really is, or is for? And where is R. D. Laing when we really need him?

As it stands, the paper contains five paragraphs and a lengthy footnote. That looks about right for a short, sharp, paradigm-shifting (Kuhn, 1970) manuscript. A few more references will serve to foster the illusion that I'm integrating ideas I've developed here with those of other theorists (Hess, 1975; Phillips & Wills, 1987; Wickes, 1958). Then, I'll insert a quotation from a great psychologist, cautioning the reader to consider "the last of the human freedoms—to choose one's attitude in any given set of circumstances" (Frankl, 1963, p. 104). Finally, with that special mixture of modesty and vision for which I fantasize I am noted, I'll conclude that the new perspectives, and intriguing, nonobvious hypotheses I have developed in this paper, should supply a generation of graduate students with opportunities for parametric extensions and conceptual replications. I trust I will be credited as second author in each.

References

Allport, G. W., & Postman, L. J. (1945). The basic psychology of rumor. *Transactions of the New York Academy of Sciences, Series II, 8,* 61–81.

Baron, R. A. (1989). *Psychology, the essential science.* Boston: Allyn & Bacon.

Bartlett, F. C. (1932). *Remembering.* Cambridge, England: Cambridge University Press.

Booth, D. A., Mather, P., & Fuller, J. (1982). Starch content of ordinary foods associatively conditions human appetite and satiation. *Appetite, 3,* 163–184.

Frankl, V. (1963). *Man's search for meaning.* New York: Washington Square Press.

Freud, S. (1908). Creative writers and daydreaming. In J. Strachey (Ed.), *Standard edition of the complete psychological works of Sigmund Freud, Vol. 9,* pp. 142–152. New York: Norton.

Hess, E. H. (1975). The role of pupil size in communication. *Scientific American,* Nov., 110–119.

Jackson, S. E., Schwab, R. L., & Schuler, R. S. (1986). Toward an understanding of the burnout phenomenon. *Journal of Applied Psychology, 71,* 630–640.

Kuhn, T. S. (1970). *The structure of scientific revolutions.* Chicago: University of Chicago Press.

Petty, R. E., & Cacioppo, J. T. (1985). The elaboration likelihood model of persuasion. In L. Berkowitz (Ed.), *Advances in experimental social psychology, Vol. 19.* New York: Academic.

Phillips, D. P., & Willis, J. S. (1987). A drop in suicides around major national holidays. *Suicide and Life-Threatening Behavior, 17,* 1–12.

Piaget, J., & Inhelder, B. (1969). *The psychology of the child.* New York: Basic Books.

Schaller, G. B. (1986). Secrets of the wild panda. *National Geographic, 169,* 284–309.

Wickes, I. G. (1958). Treatment of persistent enuresis with the electric buzzer. *Archives of Diseases in Childhood, 33,* 160–164.

Wittgenstein, L. (1958). *Philosophical investigations.* New York: Macmillan.

Understanding Your Advisor: A Survivor's Guide for Beginning Graduate Students

Alan Feingold, Ed.M.

Yale University

NEW GRADUATE STUDENTS can be easily distinguished from the more seasoned ones—the new arrivals are the ones flashing broad smiles and exuding unwarranted optimism. Beginning students like yourselves often harbor erroneous beliefs about graduate school. For example, you may associate politics with Washington—not with academic departments. Or, you may assume that the function of your advisor is to offer "advice." In graduate school, as in the business world, what you don't know can hurt you.

Success in graduate school largely depends on your ability to develop effective communication with your advisor. Unfortunately, advisors employ an argot that is confusing to most first-year students. Misunderstandings often occur between student and advisor, sometimes resulting in an abrupt and untimely end to the student's promising career. The author presents here a translation of "advisor-speak" into ordinary English, hopefully providing fledgling graduate students everywhere with the tools necessary for at least a fair chance of surviving the first year of graduate school.

What Your Advisor Says	**What Your Advisor Means**
The students in our program are competitive.	The students in our program stab one another in the back.
The students are friendly but competitive.	The students smile at one another—and then stab each other in the back.

(continued)

103

What Your Advisor Says	**What Your Advisor Means**
You're expected to live on your student stipend.	You're expected to take out thousands of dollars in loans— and still be forced to do years of teaching for us at wages that would embarrass the manager at the local McDonald's.
There are rules and regulations that must be obeyed.	There are rules and regulations that must be obeyed *by you*. The faculty can do whatever the hell we want.
You're surprisingly honest.	Boy, are you naive!
It's important that you have a powerful advisor like me to "protect you."	This department is run like a jail. Weak newcomers must quickly find a tough "protector." And you know what the price is for that protection.
Don't ever forget, I'm your advisor.	Don't ever forget, I'm your boss.
You're expected to pass a comprehensive oral examination.	This is the only exam you'll ever have to take in your life where the examiners have decided whether to pass or flunk you *before* the test has begun.
An important part of graduate education is learning to interact productively with faculty.	Graduate students must learn how to curry favor, grovel, and mindlessly concur with every prevailing belief.
If you don't follow my advice, you will have trouble getting your degree.	If you don't follow my advice, you will have trouble getting your degree.

(continued)

What Your Advisor Says	**What Your Advisor Means**
This is only a suggestion.	Of course, I can also suggest that you find another advisor.
I like the students in my class to participate in group discussion.	I "get off" on watching my students cut one another to pieces, especially now that cockfighting has been outlawed.
That's a very interesting question. Maybe we should discuss it some more—at my place.	I don't take seriously the university policy on sexual harassment.
I have tenure.	I can be tyrannical, duplicitous, and irresponsible—and nobody can do a damn thing about it.
Your paper is interesting and worthy of publication, after correction of a few crucial omissions.	My name isn't on it!
Your paper is interesting and worthy of publication, but it first needs some professional polishing.	I want to make some trivial changes—so I can justify putting my name on it.
Remember, your financial aid is provided by my grant.	Remember, if you give me any problems, you'd better be prepared to cough up 20 grand a year to continue in the program.
Your assistance on my project will afford you important research experience.	Your assistance on my project will add another publication to my vita.

(continued)

What Your Advisor Says	What Your Advisor Means
You seem to be having some problems with statistics.	Nineteen out of 20 students who displease me never get their degrees.
The department expects you to write a thesis that will make a contribution to the literature.	The department expects you to write a thesis that will take up space in the university library.
You're required to defend your thesis in an oral examination.	That's the last chance the faculty gets to take pot shots at you before granting your degree.

Understanding Your Doctoral Dissertation Committee: A Survivor's Guide for Advanced Graduate Students

D. L. Pierce, M.A.

IN A RECENT ARTICLE, Feingold (1990) demonstrated that there is a big difference between what an advisor verbalizes to his fledgling graduate student and what he really means. Feingold warned that it was the politically naive graduate student—the one who failed to pick up the latent messages of his advisor—who was most in danger of ending his own academic career prematurely. If acumen is required to correctly interpret the verbalizations and signals of the graduate advisor in the early portion of the doctoral program, then advanced techniques of translating "advisor-speak" are absolutely vital in dealing effectively with a whole committee during the most sensitive and crucial stage of the doctoral track—the oral defense of the dissertation. As a public service for graduate students everywhere, the author presents here an in-depth guide for interpreting the often enigmatic comments of the doctoral dissertation committee.

What Your Committee Says	What Your Committee Means
Look on this as a learning experience.	You're going to suffer.
Let me explain the format of the defense.	Let me waste time so you become more nervous.
We're here to support you.	We're here to destroy you so that you don't compete with us for grants and publications.

(continued)

What Your Committee Says	What Your Committee Means
I found the overall concept interesting.	This is a token compliment before I rip you to shreds.
I would have liked to have had more time to study this.	I didn't read it.
There are particular aspects of the study that I would like to hear more about.	I read it, I just don't remember it.
I have some concerns about this whole area of research.	I hate your advisor, but he/she is too powerful to insult personally so I'll use you as a proxy.
Your hypotheses were not tied to the existing literature.	You came up with a creative, new idea and we want to make sure you never do it again.
Your research is an interesting extension of my early work.	Why didn't I think of this?
You fail to take into account some relevant research.	You failed to cite my article(s).
The biological information you present does not add to an understanding of the concept.	I learned psychology in the 1950s so I don't know what you're talking about.
I'd like to point out a couple of minor inconsistencies.	I'd like to tell you in detail about every mistake you made—as well as about your shortcomings as a person.
Explain . . .	I have tenure. I don't have to think for myself.

(continued)

What Your Committee Says	**What Your Committee Means**
Your statistics do not support the hypotheses.	I don't understand anything other than a one-way ANOVA.
Your statistics are simplistic.	I'm the only one here who knows statistics and I want to rub it in.
How did you randomize your sample?	I had to come up with at least one question.
I don't think the time is right to try and publish work in this area.	At least not until I get something published in it.
Let's wrap this up.	I'm getting hungry.
Could you step out of the room so we can discuss this?	We decided beforehand to give you your Ph.D., but we want to make you sweat a bit more.

References

Feingold, A. (1990). Understanding your advisor: A survivor's guide for beginning graduate students. *Journal of Polymorphous Perversity, 7*(1), 12–14.

The Creative Employment of Typography in Identifying Specific Contributions of Various Authors to Multiple-Authored Works

Seymour Fruitlooper, Ph.D.,[1]
James C. Frankman, Ph.D.,[2]
and Tom Lowman[3]

Little Limb State College

The keen-minded journal reader generally encounters little difficulty in assessing what degree of contribution a single author has made to a scientific article when the author's name alone appears at the top of the paper. However, *this is not the case when the names of many authors appear beneath the journal article's title in what has come to be known as a "multiple-authored work."* Instead, *when faced with a multiple-authored article, the reader is left wondering just how much each author has contributed. In the past, organizations such as the American Psychological Association (APA) have suggested that the name of the chief contributor to a multiple-authored work appear first in the listing of the authors' names atop the article, with the remaining coauthors listed sequentially according to the size of their respective contributions. Most recently, the APA has drafted a code of ethics that dictates, in strong language, that scholarly credit be clearly given where it is truly due:*

> *Principal authorship and other publication credit accurately reflects the relative professional contributions of the individu-*

---

[1] *The first coauthor is Department Chair.*
[2] *The second coauthor is an untenured assistant professor.*
[3] *The third coauthor is the graduate teaching assistant of the first coauthor. This article is based on an idea provided by Michael F. Shaughnessy, Ph.D.*

> *als involved, regardless of their relative professional status.*
> *Mere possession of an institutional position such as Depart-*
> *ment Chair does not justify authorship credit. . . . Minor con-*
> *tributions to publications are acknowledged in footnotes or in*
> *an introductory statement. ("Draft of APA," 1991, p. 34)*

The coauthors of the present multiple-authored work fully concur
with the APA's admirable aim of accurately assigning author credit,
but feel the introduction of "ethics" and "ethical principles" would
largely ignore one other fairly important factor—the real world. **After**
all, *in the real world of scientific exploration and scholarly publication,*
those with academic credentials and accompanying institutional power
will ultimately find ways around ethical publication codes one way or
another. **Certainly, the Department Chair—with all of the massive**
political power that that position holds within the university set-
ting—is not going to be denied his "fair share" of articles just because
he truly invested little or no effort in helping to bring about an
experimental investigation and its subsequent report in journal article
format. *And, the lowly graduate student—the work horse of the exper-*
imental laboratory—will continue to be lowman [sic] on the academic
totem pole, largely doomed to remain in a powerless position—under-
paid, overworked, and with his name positioned last in the list of coau-
thors (no matter how great the contribution to the article).

Given the complexity of the author credit issue, **then,** *there has to*
be some form of compromise between those (like the APA) who would
demand that ethical guidelines be followed and those (like [all but one
of] the present authors) who want publishable credits to place on their
vitae and would stop at nothing (certainly not at bumping a graduate
student's name to last place in the coauthor listing) to gain such credits
as part of the prerequisite for academic (and financial) advancement.
Pressed to come up with an alternative to the APA ethical guidelines
(before the APA sets itself the task of policing the field), the present
coauthors developed a rather novel compromise: typeset the text of each
coauthor's true contributions in a different typeface, so that the reader
can readily determine precisely what each coauthor actually con-
tributed to the article. The use of such revealing typefaces will meet the
immediate ethical needs demanded by the APA of "accurately reflect[ing]
the relative professional contributions of the individuals involved." At
the same time, the coauthors' needs to pad their resumes with journal

articles will be met because the article titles and respective accompanying coauthors' names will not convey the true magnitude of the coauthors' contributions—only the body text of the articles, typeset in different typefaces, could meaningful provide such data.

The methodology of coding each coauthor's true contributions using different typefaces is fairly straightforward. Each coauthor's name is typeset in a different typeface in the coauthor listing atop the page. Then, *text attributable to any one given coauthor is typeset in the same typeface as that employed to typeset his name. (For example, the person whose name is typeset in Helvetica typeface in the coauthor listing will have all of his contributions to the text typeset in Helvetica, whereas the coauthor whose name appears in Goudy typeface will have his contributions typeset in Goudy.) On the rare occasion when two of the coauthors actually combine their writing talents and cowrite a sentence, paragraph, or passage, such mutual effort could be indicated by combining the typefaces. (For instance, if an author represented by Times Italic and another by Goudy cooperate together in writing a sentence, their mutually developed text would be typeset in Goudy Italic.)*

Sensitive to how examples can help to vividly illustrate new techniques and methodologies, the present coauthors have applied the typesetting ideas outlined in this article directly to this scholarly work in order to demonstrate the utility of our author crediting system. Now the reader can easily see the exact contribution(s) that each coauthor has made to this piece. Although it is apparent that some of the coauthors' contributions have been, at best, minimal, this does not faze any of the coauthors. After all, *as previously noted, if we cite only this published article's title on our vitae, we will have again concealed the true degree of each coauthor's contribution. It is unlikely that anyone assessing our vitae,* as we claw our way up the academic ladder, *will ever bother to dig up this article and seriously question the degree of our contribution to the piece.*

References

Draft of APA ethics code published. (1991, June). <u>APA Monitor,</u> pp. 30–35.

Advances in the Professional Psychology Internship Selection Process: The May-Kores Psychology Intern Evaluation Form

W. Ted May, Ph.D., and Robert C. Kores, Ph.D.[1]

University of Tennessee at Memphis

THE PROFESSIONAL PSYCHOLOGY internship selection process has been under much scrutiny in recent years (Candidate, 1987; Impression, 1984; Screening, Screeching, & Scrounging, 1986). Whereas the current procedure, which is oftentimes very subjective in nature, leads to frustration among intern applicants and training-site directors alike and does not necessarily lead to the "best fit" between applicants and placement sites, a more standardized and structured evaluation of the intern applicant promises to provide more reliable and valid placement. The authors present here a radically new test instrument for the evaluation and placement of prospective psychology interns.

The May-Kores Psychology Intern Evaluation Form

The May-Kores Psychology Intern Evaluation Form is employed immediately following the initial interview of the prospective intern at the internship training site. Rate the intern candidate according to the descriptors below that best fit the applicant.

---

[1] Order of authorship was determined by the randomized "rock, paper, and scissors" design.

1. Personable, thoughtful, bright, teachable, eager, and subservient. (100 points)

2. All of the above, excluding subservient. (95 points)

3. Above (#2), but including demanding. (90 points)

4. Well-trained, bright, and fairly personable. (85 points)

5. Well-trained and experienced, but anxious. (80 points)

6. Well-trained, personable, but somewhat demanding, questioning, and narcissistic. (75 points)

7. Excellent in all clinical and personal aspects, but too threatening to training staff. (70 points)

8. Educable and very eager to please. (60 points)

9. Educable clinically, but personally mediocre. (50 points)

10. Hygiene within acceptable limits. (40 points)

11. Clinically is very limited, needs too much direction, and is ugly, but has good housekeeping skills. (30 points)

12. Trainable (psychotherapeutically?). (25 points)

13. Oriented X 3. (20 points)

14. Difficulty with simultaneous walking and talking. (10 points)

15. Well-groomed, but not breathing. (5 points)

16. Breathing and psychoanalytically oriented. (1 point)

Correction Factors: The following factors, if present in the intern candidate, correct the above scores.

a. Applicant offers interviewers lunch. (+5 points)

b. Applicant picks up bar tab. (+15 points)

c. Applicant has nonclinical skills, e.g., plumbing, auto repair, babysitting, etc. (+10 points per skill)

d. Applicant has professional skills, e.g., research qualifications and willingness to accept second authorship in self-generated papers. (+25 points)

e. Applicant in three-piece suit. (−30 points)

f. Applicant has punk haircut, moussed purple, with safety pin through cheek. (No minus points for haircut, but −5 points per pin)

g. Applicant plans *local* private practice following completion of internship. (−50 points)

Total Points (Subtotal Points + Correction Factor): _____

Scoring Key

Total Points	Training-Site Director's Decision
0 or less	Reject applicant
1–49	Offer 2nd alternate
50–99	Offer 1st alternate
100–149	Accept applicant
150 or more	*Kidnap* applicant

Further Research

The authors invite other researchers to assess the reliability and validity of The May-Kores Psychology Intern Evaluation Form. The authors are confident that this new, state-of-the-art test instrument will stand up well, particularly when compared with more traditional methods of intern selection, e.g., subjective selection procedures and flipping of coins.

References

Candidate, P. (1987). The measurement and generation of psychology intern cripples. *Archives of Abnormal Psychology, 34,* 895–901.

Impression, T. (1984). Scrutiny issues in the process of selection. *Journal of Criminal Investigation and Practice, 44,* 10–20.

Screening, B., Screeching, B., & Scrounging, B. (1986). The reliability of psychology internship selection practices. *Journal of the Psychology Bulletin, 13,* 45–84.

Further Advances in the Professional Psychology Internship Selection Process: Interpretive Guidelines for Letters of Reference

Harry L. Piersma, Ph.D.

Pine Rest Christian Hospital

IN A RECENT *JPP* article, May and Kores (1989) proposed several new standards for evaluating prospective psychology interns. The present article supplements these standards with interpretive guidelines for applicants' letters of reference. It is commonly agreed (Piersma, 1990) that reference letters may be misleading, if their content is interpreted literally. One reason for this is that individuals who write reference letters generally want to assist interns in gaining desired placements. However, most reference writers also have a (usually unconscious) desire to be honest, and want to let internship site interviewers know about particular deficit areas a candidate may have. But delineating these deficit areas in a clear and understandable manner may hurt an individual's application. The result of this ethical quandary is usually vague candidate descriptions, open to broad interpretation, with applicants' deficiencies typically understated.

The following guidelines have developed out of the author's own continual struggle to figure out how the given person described in a reference letter bears any resemblance whatsoever to the person who sits before him in the selection interview. Like most everything in our field, these guidelines are subject to further research and probable disconfirmation.

What the Reference Letter Says	What the Reference Letter Means
She has developed an active counseling style.	Her clients rarely are able to get in a word edgewise.
Her maturity is complemented by humor, solidity, and steadiness of purpose.	She really is a bore, but I did see her smile once.
His verbal skills are stronger than his writing skills.	His masters thesis was damn near unintelligible.
There are those who are flashier . . .	. . . he had been in my class for a year before he said a word.
She is very open to the supervisory process.	She agreed with even my most inept suggestions.
He has an underlying humility . . .	. . . but is overtly obnoxious.
She is a pleasure to supervise and a joy with whom to work.	She treats me with the deference and respect that I deserve.
His clinical work is typified by his quiet, thoughtful style.	I don't know whether I would classify him as schizoid, but he's close.
We have been impressed with her introspective nature and quiet inner strength.	She seems to be a troubled person, but she never bothers anybody with her problems.
She is somewhat resistant to the heavy demands of record-keeping and administrative requirements.	She never turned in a single report on time, even when I made an issue of it in supervision.

(continued)

What the Reference Letter Says	What the Reference Letter Means
We found her personal style to be task-oriented.	Her ability to relate to clients on an affectual level was zilch.
He has identified materials that I have used in my own research and writing.	He has written articles for me, and does not ask for even footnote recognition.
He has a somewhat intellectualized approach to therapy.	He is incredibly out of touch with both his own and his clients' feelings.
She is by no means a doormat . . .	. . . though she easily passes for one.
In comparison to other graduate students, this person is in the top 1%.	She may be a little better than the average student.
. . . top 5%.	Generally, she is a very mediocre student.
. . . top 10%.	He was voted least likely to succeed by his peers.
. . . top 25%.	We wonder how we ever accepted this person into our program, given his failure to outscore an apple on the WAIS–R.
. . . top 50%.	This person is said to have emitted an intelligible phrase once, although the report came from his mother.

References

May, W. T., & Kores, R. C. (1989). Advances in the professional psychology internship selection process: The May-Kores Psychology Intern Evaluation Form. *Journal of Polymorphous Perversity, 6*(2), 14–15.

Piersma, H. L. (1990). The generalizability of the opinions of me, myself, and I. *Journal of Consensual Validation, 1*(1), 1.

A Kübler-Rossian Analysis of the Stages of Self-Deception in the Completion of Masters and Doctoral Theses

D. W. Sehy, M.S.

University of Illinois at Urbana

RESEARCH HAS SHOWN that a suitable masters or doctoral candidate proceeds through definite and identifiable psychological stages during the writing of a thesis or dissertation. Retrospective population studies have highlighted five discrete psychological stages that closely parallel those identified by Kübler-Ross (1969): denial/avoidance, anger/resentment, delusion, angst, and acceptance.

I. Denial / Avoidance

Denial

This stage can be diagnosed by the candidate's use of such phrases as, "Thesis? What is this thing called thesis?" and "Lots of people—decent, kind, honest, hardworking people—get non-thesis masters degrees."

The Denial Stage candidate may decide that an advanced degree is really not his personal "style." In fact, he might decide that, being so used to living at the poverty level, he could not be comfortable with the reasonable income tenuously associated with the completion of a graduate degree. The candidate consoles himself further: "Minimum wage jobs are *really quite liberating;* they keep a person out of the Capitalistic Rat Race." With this perspective, the candidate can even claim a moral victory over the majority of the rest of society. After all, most are motivated by superficial desires such as decent shelter, sufficient food, and warm clothing. By staying out of the real work force, the candidate believes he will do humankind a service—akin to joining the Peace Corps but without the inconvenience of contracting some tropical illness characterized by "explosive diarrhea."

A candidate who becomes fixated upon the Denial Stage may eventually find himself saying such things as, "Hi. I am Dave and I will *appear* to be your waiter this evening. However, I am actually *not* your waiter; rather I am playing the role of waiter in tonight's performance of 'The Waiter,' produced, written, directed by, and starring me, Dave. You are the audience participating in my interactive, synergistic, cybernetic personal drama. Now, during the course of this Meal Performance kindly remember that, as *The Artist,* I will be free to creatively interpret your orders. Also, please note that my work is not supported by any State or Federal Arts Council grant monies, so feel free to tip as if your lives depend on it. Thank you. Now on to Act I. I'd like to recommend the sockeye salmon in lemon and butter sauce. . . ."

Avoidance

A behavior pattern concomitant to the Denial Stage is Avoidance. This behavior is characterized by procrastination of an increasingly complex and sophisticated nature such that three subphases of Avoidance can be identified: simple, creative, and desperately creative.

In *Simple Avoidance* the candidate may practice any or all of the following harmless self-deceptions and behaviors: "As soon as I finish listening to this ten-cassette subliminal audiotape series on 'Ending Procrastination Within My Lifetime,' I will *definitely* have my last cup of coffee, clean the kitchen, do the grocery shopping, dust the bottoms of the chairs, *and then I'll get straight to work on that explosive, controversial third subsection of the Introduction. I really mean it.* But wait a moment. A work of this magnitude requires—no, demands—intense introspection and self-critique if it's to be done at all." And as creative enthusiasm and distorted reality begin to dominate the psyche ". . . Yes, damn it. I don't want to pander to the sensibilities of my audience, I want to challenge them. This thesis has lost all social relevance. Perhaps I just need a new direction. A new medium for Ultimate Communication. A communion of enlightenment mediated *by me.* Perhaps there is still time to adapt my Results section into a gritty, realist drama, or at least an embittered performance art piece with angst written all over it. My Materials and Methods sections could become my magnum opus if I just transform it into sonnet form."

Creative Avoidance is a slightly more complex behavior pattern rooted in the socially instilled urges to "do something, anything" as long as such activities are not a reminder of The Real Task. The candidate can rationalize the need to undertake remotely worthy alternative jobs. For example, the candidate may find himself renewing friendships, canning vegetables, relearning geometric proofs, conjugating French irregular verbs, or designing the ultimate Karaoke bar. The candidate might look for a lucrative side-line career and start freelancing as a literary and arts critic. He might begin by practicing with phrases like, "I admired its *devastating reality* and *uncompromising honesty. A literary triumph;* I laughed, I cried."

Desperately Creative Avoidance is a rare and extreme category of avoidance behaviors, probably typified by the author's writing of this article. A particularly striking example of this advanced behavior pattern is *death.* In this instance, a candidate succumbs to internal voices urging him to take the easiest way out, thus obviating the need for countless rewrites and tedious minor changes to the body of the first draft.

II. Anger / Resentment

The "What is Thesis?" Delusion

A common transitional mode from Denial/Avoidance to Anger/Resentment involves a period of extreme self-doubt and uncertainty about the *true nature of the world,* in other words, "College Philosophy Flashback." Following in the footsteps of Descartes, the candidate charges that no work on the abstract concept of "thesis" will be done until such time as the true "being-ness" of said thesis is demonstrated in "clear and distinct" terms, based on first principles. "What can I know of an abstraction such as 'thesis,' when the existence of the chair upon which I perceive myself to sit has not even been proven?" the candidate ponders. With extreme rationality the candidate will decide, "First, I must establish a criterion for Truth, then I will prove my own existence *(cog-*

ito ergo sum), then the existence of this chair *(cogito ergo sum office furniture)*, then the *a priori* existence of God, and then I'll have another coffee, and *then I'll get straight to work on the results section. I really mean it this time."*

Once the futility of such reasoning is realized, the candidate enters the Anger/Resentment stage with an attitude of cautious agnosticism: "I may exist and, if my existence is real, why would my perceptions deceive me about the existence of this chair, and though God's existence is irrelevant, 'thesis' will be assumed to exist within my realm of understanding until such time as I receive further evidence to disprove its existence or I win the lottery."

Once the *possibility* of the existence of a thesis has been established, the Anger/Resentment stage degree candidate may examine the actual duties associated with such a concept. At this point the candidate may proceed to furiously shuffle papers around for a few minutes before resolving that he can go no further until one particular journal article is found, stamp around the room looking for it for 25 minutes, then call it a day. Best to get a fresh start in the morning.

The next day, seeing the huge stack of journals before him, the candidate is momentarily daunted, but stoically presses on, in alphabetical order of course, since *Modern Pornography* and *National Enquirer* must precede *Science* in sequence. Weeks later, when the candidate feels sufficiently familiar with the literature, he turns to the huge stack of scientific journals piled before him and neurons fire desperately to formulate the next Thesis Escape Mechanism.

III. Delusion

Delusion is the phase in which the candidate confuses his fantastic and imagined notions about the job at hand with the Reality of The Task. This may come in the form of a regression to past experience, creating a delusion such as: "With enough paper, pencils, coffee, and a set of World Book Encyclopedias, one all-nighter at the IHOP should take care of this sucker." The relatively harmless, but expensive, lottery delusion is common: "If I can just win the Lotto, I won't have to finish; I just need to figure out a system."

Alternately, delusions may be of an aggressive and violent nature, aimed at imagined perpetrators of a conspiracy against the candidate.

This condition is affectionately known as *The Streleski Psychosis*. The following are progressively more severe delusions:

> If my roommate kills himself, I'll get an A, and won't have to finish.
>
> If I kill my roommate, I'll get an A and won't have to finish.
>
> If I kill my advisor, I'll get an A and won't have to finish.
>
> If I kill everyone in the department, I'll get an A and I'll never have to wear my high school PE uniform again.

And then there's the most advanced delusion:

> If I just drink the blood of three tenured faculty members in a clandestine ceremony, I'll achieve enlightenment without the tedium of doing several low-paying academic post-docs, and I still won't have to wear my high school PE uniform ever again.

Delusions of a medical nature are also quite common and often reveal hypochondriacal features:

> Perhaps lack of motivation and a nonexistent attention span are symptoms of a *serious degenerative nerve disease*. If I only have months to live, is this how I want to spend my Final Days?!
>
> How can I be sure that eight times the recommended daily allowance of fiber is really enough?
>
> Either my biorhythms have gone critical or my Seasonal Affective Disorder is acting up again.
>
> As long as I'm eating right I'll be able to cope with the incredible stress of the task; let's see, today I've had something from the Caffeine Group, the Artificial Sweetener Group, the Non-Dairy Dairy Products Group, the Fiber Group, the Non-Aspirin Pain-Relievers Group, the Fermented Hops Beverage Group, and the Flintstone Vitamins Group. I should be O.K.

IV. Angst

Angst is a highly complex emotion/behavior formerly felt only by Artis*tes* and reactionaries who would walk around saying things like, *"Things are* the *way they* are," with oddly placed accents. Angst is a sort of artistic brooding phenomenon now felt by the general public, though less commonly outside of academia. Clove cigarettes, black pointy shoes, and really expensive T-shirts are not required to enjoy angst, but proper costuming does add to a desirable ambience. Feelings of angst are heightened by consumption of over-priced Italian coffee in smokey, stylized coffee shops.

At this point the candidate realizes the importance of letting any passing stranger know how incredibly tough it is to write a thesis (though inwardly acknowledging, "it's tougher with a family"). Each page becomes a ritual of melodrama, wherein the candidate stretches his dramatic abilities to the limits to express the stomach-churning agony of copying things from a book onto a page, while taking coffee breaks every 5 minutes. This is the stage at which it becomes important for the candidate to work in places such as coffee shops, where he will have greater opportunity to express publicly the *intensely private* inner conflict associated with a monumental task such as the writing of a thesis.

Also associated with Angst is the sort of literary enlightenment that gives the candidate the freedom to spend hours deciding whether to choose the verb "use" or "utilize" in scientific writing. The candidate will painstakingly weigh the options in terms of contextual sincerity and creative integrity. He will constantly chide himself: "Does this sentence about HLA-DRA gene expression really connote the feelings I have here and now about World Peace and the Rights of Human Beings to pursue their destiny with freedom and dignity? How can I say this without altering the explicit meaning of the sentence?"

In a late-night fit of artistic and literary pique, the candidate vows to write only with *exceptional insight, sensitivity, clarity, and heightened consideration for the emotional needs of the readers*. With frantic determination, the candidate goes back through the entire document changing any gender-implicating pronouns to androgynous references. The candidate meticulously replaces the *offensive, sexist term* for cell scraper, "rubber policeman," with the more liberating and humanitarian "rubber policeperson" everywhere he encounters it. With tears of joy and pride streaming down his face, he claims *a major victory for feminism and modern progressive thought.* The candidate then takes the rest of the day off to reflect on the keenness of insight and depth of sensitivity to the human condition he expressed, and to wish more people were so enlightened.

V. Acceptance

Once the first draft of the thesis has somehow been thrown together, the candidate succumbs to the final stage—a sort of fatalistic Acceptance. In the end, he concedes, "Maybe there is an actual entity outside of my existence but within my perception that resembles the concept of thesis, as I have been led to understand it. It is not complete, merely a rough draft, but it appears to be as real as this chair upon which I sit (though that is no great consolation)."

References

Kübler-Ross, E. (1969). *On death and dying.* NY: Macmillan.

The Tenure System in Higher Education: A Case Study

Diana Conway, Ph.D.

University of Alaska at Anchorage

IN THE BEGINNING God created heaven and earth. And God made two great lights: the greater light to rule the day, and the lesser light to rule the night. And God created great whales, and every living creature that moveth. And God said, Let us make man in our image, after our likeness; male and female created He them. And on the seventh day God ended His work which He had made and applied for tenure.

The Dean of the College of Arts and Sciences of Universal University balanced God's tenure file in his hand as he spoke. "I see you have completed the prerequisite time at our university for tenure, but I'm not sure you meet all the basic requirements."

"Have I not made heaven and earth, the stars of the firmament, the living creatures, and so on?" asked God.

"Oh, I'm not questioning your public service, which is, as you point out, quite extensive. But I see no evidence of teaching expertise. Why don't you concentrate on your teaching and reapply later?"

God returned to Eden somewhat humbled by the interview. In order to perfect His teaching, He created the tree of knowledge of good and evil in the midst of the garden and told Adam and Eve that they might freely eat of any tree except that one. His instructional objective was to teach self-restraint. Unfortunately, His pupils failed their first test and had to be expelled from school.

God decided to formulate a clear set of expected student behaviors, which he delivered to Moses on Mt. Sinai. The student success rate at meeting those objectives was fairly low. God then tried various incentive programs as well as punishments based on logical consequences (e.g., floods, turning to salt in the desert, exclusion from the Promised Land, etc.) and He at last found His star pupil in Job. For Job survived all the tests and repented of his doubt, and he was rewarded by God with 7 sons, 3 daughters, 14,000 sheep, and an A. And God reactivated His application for tenure.

Dr. Peter Haisley, Chair of the Humanities Division Peer Review Committee, set God's expanded file on the table and tapped it gingerly with the tips of his fingers. "This committee is quite impressed with your recent successes in teaching," he said. "In addition, we find your public service to be above the level needed for nomination to tenure." Dr. Haisley cleared his throat and continued with some obvious distress. "However, the third aspect on which we must judge you is publication. Unfortunately, we find no evidence of your scholarly writing."

God looked at the floor and replied in a meek voice, "I've been terribly busy keeping up with day to day management of the world. There just never seems to be enough time to get to research."

The Chair nodded sympathetically. "Please don't let our findings discourage you. We think you are a potentially excellent candidate for tenure. Shall we count on seeing you next time around then?"

God wondered as He left the room why He found these minor professional setbacks so humiliating.

Since only publication stood between God and tenure, He immediately called His Teaching Assistants together and bade them begin preliminary research. Acting as they were under divine inspiration, it didn't take long for them to have separate drafts on His desk. God praised them all for their efforts. He was particularly proud of Matthew, Mark, Luke, and John for creating stylistic variants of similar text. God quickly made an appointment with the Campus Wide Tenure Review Committee.

The Gideon Society copies of the Old and New Testaments, bound in black leather embossed with gilt lettering, lay on the table between God and Dr. Carl Letterer. "I'm sorry to disappoint you once again," he began, "but the Campus Wide Tenure Review Committee does not believe these publications to be sufficient to warrant tenure."

For the first time since the beginning of the arduous approval process, God began to feel more choleric than chagrined. "Exactly what is wrong with them?" He demanded to know.

"It's a matter of citations," answered Dr. Letterer, unconsciously stepping back from the gleam in God's granite eyes. "You see, we can only accept scholarly work from refereed journals or publishing houses. Don't take this in the wrong way. As a preliminary draft, these works are outstanding. Now, if you'd just give credit to your predecessors."

"Predecessors!" thundered God. "My career work is entirely original."

"Oh come now," answered Dr. Letterer with an ironic little smile barely creasing the corners of his mouth. "What about your colleagues Zeus, Hera, Poseidon, Athena? It's a simple matter of a few judicious footnotes standing between you and tenure. I'm sure you can fix things up by the next time we meet."

God leaned heavily against the table and mentally counted to ten. He imagined earthquake, fire, and flood, but in the end settled for a simpler solution.

"I resign," He said. God turned His back on the committee, walked majestically out the door, turned the corner, followed the hall to the main portal, and left Universal University forever.

Relief From the Publish-or-Perish Dilemma: How to Count Articles in Dubious Journals as Professional Publication Credits

Sandra K. Trisdale

University of Louisville

IN THE PUBLISH-OR-PERISH (or occasionally publish-and-perish-any-way) world of academia, it is crucial to have as many publications as possible on one's vita. Unfortunately, many social scientists have not yet learned that anything can be counted as a professional publication if presented convincingly. In the present paper, the author offers simple and effective guidelines for fattening one's vita with manuscripts that one may have finally succeeded in getting published, albeit in dubious journals—while giving the impression that these publications are scholarly in nature. Advanced techniques for maintaining this illusion while being scrutinized by the job interviewer are also presented.

Techniques for Counting Publications in Dubious Journals

Technique #1: Abbreviate

Most social scientists like to use initials in referring to journals. They throw around "JAMA" and "JCC" so much that you'd think they owned the things. So do the same on your vita. For example, *Journal of Polymorphous Perversity* becomes *JPP,* which sounds quite respectable. If you prefer, you can "creatively" abbreviate, so that *Journal of Polymorphous Perversity* becomes *Jnl Pm Per,* which, with any luck, may be mistaken for something like *Journal of Postmortem Personality* (referring, of course, to the science of analyzing cadavers). It sounds good, and that's the important thing!

Technique #2: Have No Shame

Need a publication? You have plenty lying around that you can use. For example, that joke you stole from an old comedy routine for which *Reader's Digest* paid you 300 dollars, the one about the wine, the preacher, and the Ten Commandments. You would cite this on your vita as:

> Smith, J. (1988). The effects of ethyl alcohol and anxiety on the long-term memory of higher members of the Protestant clergy. *RD, 3,* 17.

Other material that can be used in this fashion includes letters to the editor, winning bake-off recipes, Hints to Heloise, letters to Dear Abby or Ann Landers, and for the truly shameless, graffiti.

Advanced Techniques for Maintaining the Illusion of Scholarly Works During the Job Interview

Advanced Technique #1: Go on the Offensive

If applying for a job, begin by saying, "Now, of course, you've read my paper on alcoholism and the clergy in *RD,* haven't you?" With any luck, the interviewer will be too embarrassed to deny it.

Advanced Technique #2: Have a Faked Illness Ready

If asked exactly what journal *PBN (Pillsbury Bake-Off Newsletter)* is, be prepared to go into an instant, convincing, and prolonged coughing spell, at the end of which you say, "Now, what were we discussing? Oh, yes. My dissertation. Now let me explain it to you in depth . . ."

The fake beepers you can purchase (the ones where you touch a button and it beeps you a couple of seconds later) are good for those social scientists with delicate throats, or those who have a lot of job interviews lined up.

Advanced Technique #3: Be Clumsy

Knocking over the interviewer's coffee onto your vita can be a good move if you're backed into a corner. Similarly, judicious "smearing" before the vita goes out can help a lot.

Advanced Technique #4: Sandwich the Publication Carefully

To the extent that you can manage, try to have at least two legitimate publications for every dubious one. For instance, your letter that was published in *Penthouse* (the one about you and the Eskimo and the penguin when you went on vacation, titled in your vita "Unusual Sexual Proclivities Among Northern Native Americans and Aptenodytes Patagonica") should be mixed in with your research on whether it is better that psychologists' office walls are painted white or off-white.

Conclusion

So there you have it. With only a little creativity, a lot of gall, and a complete disregard for the American Psychological Association's code of ethics, you can pad your vita and be the envy of your department. In fact, the author plans to make judicious use of the present article (which, of course, appears as you read this in *Jnl Pm Per,6*(2), 21–22) in updating her own vita.

The author wishes you good luck in the successful application of the aforementioned techniques. Please note that the author's usual fee is 10% of the salary you get in your new job, with an added 5% if it gets you tenure.

8

Experimental
Psychology

B. F. and I

Lawrence Casler, Ph.D.

State University of New York at Geneseo

SO FAR AS I KNOW, B. F. Skinner did not dedicate any of his books to me, and my name does not appear in any of his acknowledgments. In view of our many interactions, I find these omissions hard to understand.

It all began in the early 1950s. I was an undergraduate, an English major, and I needed a science course to satisfy a "distribution" requirement. Nat. Sci. 114 fit nicely into my schedule, and the catalog description made the course sound less onerous than the others that were available. I had never heard of B. F. Skinner, but by the same (or a very similar) token, he had probably never heard of me. Despite this mutual ignorance, the course turned out to be moderately entertaining. The highlight was the table tennis game played by two pigeons. I remember rooting for the one on the left. In retrospect, I should have chosen the other one—the one whose wicked cross-court shots creamed the opponent. Being very intelligent in those days, I immediately realized that the point of this performance was not the game itself but rather the demonstration of techniques that could be applied for other purposes. "If pigeons can be taught to play Ping-Pong," I asked myself, "what other games can they be taught to play?"

My acumen notwithstanding, I did not distinguish myself in the course, ending up with some kind of B. (Terminological note: People who say they received "some kind of B" really mean B − . If they received a B, they would say, "I got a B." If they earned a B + , they would say, "I got a B + " or "an A − .") I remember losing points because I didn't understand the difference between punishment and negative reinforcement. This confusion, I now realize, should not have been a cause of embarrassment. There I was, a mere beginner, already functioning at the exalted level of most introductory textbook authors.

I asked only one question during the course. Skinner had just asserted that motivation is merely a behavioral tendency. I raised my hand and asked, "Does that mean that the only way I can know if a man is hungry is to see him eat?" I suspect that Skinner had heard the question before, but he answered without a hint of condescension: "No, verbalizations can usually be trusted. If he says he's hungry, he's probably hungry." That interchange, brief though it was, served the double function of being both the first and last of our conversations.

Our paths next crossed a year or so later. I was in attendance at a debate (not *the* debate, but *a* debate) between Skinner and Carl Rogers. What I found most impressive was that these two great men (I knew they were great because of the large audience they drew and because of the loud laughter that was elicited by even the mildest of their jests) really seemed to like each other. In those days, I thought a debate had to have a winner. I picked Rogers, not based on the quality of his logic, but because I preferred his assumptions. In retrospect, I should have chosen Skinner.

Years passed before our life paths were to intersect again. After graduating with a degree in English literature, I had decided to make the Big Switch to psychology. (Students of the intellectual history of the Western World will immediately note the similarity in this regard between B. F. and the present author.) First there was my psychoanalytic stage, during which I thought Freud was the be-all and end-all. Then came my Skinnerian stage. I often went to hear my ex-teacher speak at American Psychological Association conventions, especially when the topic was something elusive like consciousness. Through the years, I invariably concluded that what he had to say on such topics was more interesting than what his critics said and more interesting than what his critics said he said. (I suppose that is why I am still in my Skinnerian stage.)

One of the conventions I attended included a paper-reading session at which I noticed B. F. sitting in the audience, just like a regular person. In the discussion period following an account of certain aversive procedures that had reduced the self-reported rate of smoking, I suggested that the subjects might have lied either because they wanted to please or impress the investigators or because they wanted to avert further aversives. Skinner was just a few rows in front of me, and I could see him nod in agreement. Only the dignity of my position as Assistant Professor prevented me from rushing over and suggesting that maybe it wasn't too late for him to change my grade to a straight B.

I have reported that B. F. and I did not engage in any conversations after my question and his answer in Nat. Sci. 114, but that doesn't mean we stopped exchanging words. In the early 1970s, I had written a book, and my publisher and I thought that a Foreword by Skinner would be a good thing. Accordingly, I sent a brief summary and a polite request. His response was prompt and courteous. (I have learned that one way to distinguish between really important people and those who merely think they are important is that the former answer their mail.) His response was also negative. He regretted that the pressure of his work made it necessary for him to decline nearly all such requests.

All good things must come to an end, and it was at that point that he and I ceased being pen pals. Always the gentleman, he never presumed to take up my time by asking for advice concerning some of the subtler aspects of behavior analysis, even though I am quite sure I would have been willing to interrupt my busy schedule in order to give him a few pointers.

So there you have it. It should be obvious by now that my impact on B. F.'s personal life was equaled only by my impact on his research. (Actually, as our relationship deepened through the years, I stopped thinking of him as "B. F." To me, he became simply "B." Presumably, to him, I remained "B − .")

What is the explanation, one must ask, for his strange silence concerning the extent of my influence? Professional jealousy? No, he was above such things. Forgetfulness? Not likely. I have no choice but to conclude that my importance to him was of such a nature that he preferred to keep it to himself.

Effects of Cultural Sensitivity on Self and Ethnic Identity and Select Demographic Characteristics of Hispanic Adolescents

Roberto G. Malgadi, Ph.D.[1]

New York University

CENSUS STATISTICS for 1970 and 1980, coupled with advance 1990 reports, suggest that the Hispanic population in the United States is growing at such a rate that early in the next century virtually all Americans will be Hispanic. Although it is difficult to reliably estimate the number (and hence population proportion) of illegal Hispanic residents in this country, at any given time there are actually even more Hispanics than census figures indicate. Taken together, this implies that more than all Americans will be Hispanic in the next century. Sociological and demographic theories provide insight into this phenomenon, attributing rapid Hispanic population growth to three factors: immigration from Latin America, increased birth rates associated with marriage of Hispanics not only to other Hispanics but also to non-Hispanics, and Hispanic fertility and mortality rates indicating that Hispanics tend to reproduce before dying (Rogler, Malgady, & Rodriguez, 1989).

The rapid growth in the Hispanic population is alarming to professional psychology because epidemiological evidence suggests that although Hispanics have higher prevalence rates of *DSM-III-R* disorders, they tend to underutilize traditional mental health services (Rodriguez, 1987). If such trends persist, as more people become Hispanic, fewer will use the services of psychologists. One way to preempt the

---

[1] This is a culturally sensitive spelling of the author's name.

prospect of a clientele void for psychologists in the next century is to heed the message of those who have called for culturally sensitive psychotherapeutic services (e.g., Rogler, Malgady, Costantino, & Blumenthal, 1987; Sue, 1988). At the broadest level of conceptualization, culturally sensitive services attempt to implement innovative psychological techniques to eradicate barriers to utilization of community mental health services. Some new techniques that have an empirically documented impact on utilization rates include: having Spanish-speaking personnel communicate with Hispanic clients who speak little or no English; maintaining a culturally congruent ambiance (e.g., pictures of palm trees in the psychiatric emergency room); locating services in the center of the *barrio,* thus overcoming the accessibility barriers posed by costly public transportation and by private transportation, which requires an ability to read English road signs in order to get around.

More refined definitions of cultural sensitivity pertain to what actually transpires during the therapeutic process. Prior to mass migration of Hispanics to the U.S., Freud (1927) was perhaps the first to recognize early on that unacculturated Hispanics in Vienna ($N = 2$) were not good candidates for long-term, intensive, and costly insight-oriented therapy. More effective treatment modalities have been family therapy (e.g., Malgady, Rogler, & Costantino, 1990). The purpose of the present study was to examine treatment outcomes in a program of culturally sensitive modeling therapy with Hispanic adolescents. This study investigated the effects of cultural modeling on self and ethnic identification, and selected demographic factors known from epidemiological research to place adolescents at risk of mental disorder.

Method

Subjects

The subjects were 55 second-generation (U.S. born) adolescents (age 12–15), largely of Puerto Rican descent, recruited from an inner-city public school in Brooklyn, New York. In order to maximize the rate of voluntary participation, informed consent was secured in English from their first-generation, monolingual Spanish-speaking parents. The cultural specificity of treatment effects was examined by including a comparable group of 55 White adolescents, who were recruited from a private school in Westchester County, New York.

Procedures

Subjects were randomly assigned to one of two conditions: culturally sensitive modeling therapy or an attention video-control group. Each treatment condition was administered in a community mental health center after school hours to maximize attendance, since school attendance rates were below 50% in the Puerto Rican sample and above 100% in the White sample. Hourly (50 min) sessions were conducted for 12 weeks on a small group basis ($n = 0$ to 5 members per group).

In the experimental intervention, subjects were exposed to biographies of famous Puerto Rican role models of achievement (e.g., Geraldo Rivera) to instill a sense of self-esteem, ethnic awareness, and adaptive coping with adverse demographic characteristics. Each week a different role model was presented, and sociodramatic play followed a discussion of each biography in order to provide a therapeutic vehicle for reinforcement of imitative behavior.

In the video-control condition, subjects were exposed to noncultural traditional play therapy (e.g., Pac-man, Super-Mario Brothers, Asteroids). Sessions alternated between individual and team competition.

Outcome Measures

Subjects were pre- and posttested with a battery of treatment outcome measures. Self identification (S-ID) was measured objectively by code numbers ranging from 001 to 110 ($M = 55.5$). This measurement procedure is widely used in research with human subjects to ensure confidentiality (National Institute of Mental Health, 1976). The S-ID scores were assigned in the subject's preferred language (e.g., "uno" or "one"). Test-retest reliability of S-ID scores was adequate for research purposes ($r > .70$, $p < .001$).

Ethnic identification (E-ID) was measured by self-report rating on a 5-point scale in response to the question: "How Puerto Rican do you feel?" Ratings ranged from "1" (not at all Puerto Rican) to "5" (extremely

Puerto Rican). Internal consistency *(alpha)* reliability of this item was perfect.

Demographic risk factors included critical adolescent developmental period (age), urban/suburban residential status (dummy coded), monthly family income (in dollars), parental socioeconomic status (SES; 1–7 Hollingshead Scale rating), and number of mentally ill persons in household (as recorded by standardized interviews).

Results

The data were analyzed as a pretest-posttest, ethnicity × experimental-control group design with multiple outcome measures. A two-way multivariate analysis of covariance (MANCOVA) was conducted (with pretest scores as covariates), which revealed a significant interaction effect, $F(7,89) = 34.12$, $p < .001$. The omnibus MANCOVA was followed by univariate ANCOVAs with Pepperoni protection of family-wise Type I error rate.

The ANCOVA of S-ID scores revealed that the mean of the experimental group ($M = 83$) was significantly higher than the mean ($M = 28$) of the control group, $F(1, 105) = 1064.69$, $p < .001$, and there was no significant interaction. Thus, culturally sensitive intervention significantly enhanced the self identification of adolescents, regardless of their ethnicity. The ANCOVA of E-ID scores revealed a strong ordinal ethnicity × treatment interaction, $F(1, 105) = 24.46$, $p < .001$. Puerto Rican adolescents in the culturally sensitive intervention felt more Puerto Rican ($M = 4.5$) than their Puerto Rican cohorts in the control condition ($M = 3.5$); however, White adolescents were even more likely to feel highly Puerto Rican ($M = 4.2$) compared with their ethnic controls ($M = 1.0$).

The analysis of impact of demographic risk factors produced mixed findings. Regarding developmental risk, it was found that all groups aged the same extent during the 12 week intervention period, all $Fs = 0$, $ps > .9999$. Although this does not prove the null hypothesis, power analysis suggests if the study is replicated with $N = \infty$, the probability of Type II error would indeed be less.

Log-linear analysis applied to residential status, which was dichotomously scored (urban = 1, suburban = 0), revealed a significant treatment x ethnicity interaction ($p < .001$). There was no difference among

Puerto Rican treatment groups (all still lived in Brooklyn), but 57% of the White subjects in culturally sensitive treatment forced their parents to move to Brooklyn, whereas their controls remained in suburbia.

The ANCOVAs of family income and SES each revealed only a main effect due to ethnicity: income $F(1, 105) = 1760.89$, $p < .001$; SES $F(1, 105) = 440.40$, $p < .001$. Controlling for pretest differences and regardless of treatment group, Puerto Rican families were still significantly poorer ($M = \$1,258$ monthly) and of lower SES ($M = 2.6$) after the intervention compared with their White counterparts (M income $= \$5,469$ monthly; M SES $= 6.7$).

Finally, the ANCOVA of the contagion risk factor (number of mentally ill family members) revealed a slight but significant disordinal interaction effect, $F(1, 105) = 4.01$, $p < .05$). Puerto Ricans in culturally sensitive treatment had fewer mentally ill household members than Puerto Rican control subjects; the predominant psychiatric symptomatology of control families was visual hallucinations. However, cross-cultural specificity was demonstrated among White families, in which there were significantly more mentally ill family members associated with the cultural modeling intervention. Post hoc analysis revealed that this effect was correlated with post-treatment residential status and E-ID scores: White subjects who reported feeling highly Puerto Rican and who moved to Brooklyn had significantly more family members suffering from delusional symptomatology (during debriefing, many reported *being* Geraldo). An incidental finding was that, regardless of *DSM-III-R* disorder, there were significantly more members of Puerto Rican families than White families.

Discussion

Most compelling among the present findings is the impact of culturally sensitive modeling therapy on self and ethnic identity, two critical factors influencing adjustment during the turbulent adolescent years (Confused, 1983 or 1984). In attempting to replicate these findings with other populations, it is important to code control group subjects' confidential ID numbers in a computer data file before the experimental group subjects. Furthermore, in cross-cultural research if a main effect due to ethnicity is sought, S-ID scores should be coded arbitrarily lower for one ethnic group than another.

The cross-cultural modeling effect on ethnic identity was, frankly, a serendipitous finding. However, this may have preventive mental health value. Given the census projections cited earlier, the White subjects who increased their Puerto Rican identity will be better prepared to face life as Hispanics during the next century. Similarly, the cross-cultural residential effect localized among Whites has a preventive mental health function. Although this may appear to be a negative treatment outcome, since urban residence is a high risk indicator, when Whites move from the suburbs to inner-city communities, they have a greater probability of socialization and, ultimately, intermarriage with bonafide Hispanics. Therefore, they will be better prepared to behave in a manner consistent with Hispanic majority normative standards, and they will be more likely to have Hispanic children.

There are serious implications for community mental health planning of the contagion effects found among nonparticipating family members in the present study. The dilemma is that video-play therapy can induce visual hallucinations among family members, and on the other hand, crossing cultures can induce delusions of being a Puerto Rican talk show host. As both outcomes are *DSM-III-R* diagnostic criteria of schizophrenia, modeling and play therapy ought to be implemented as family modalities.

The lack of statistical significance of age effects may at first blush appear disheartening. However, this demonstrates that treatment intervention neither accelerates nor impedes the developmental process. Caution must be exercised, once again, because this conclusion is tantamount to accepting the null hypothesis (Logic & Fisher, 1923).

References

Confused, I. M. (1983 or 1984). Optical resolution of the adolescent identity crisis. *Journal of Developmental Perception, 12,* 3.

Freud, S. (1927). *Hispanos en sicoterapia analitica: Una modalidad que no trabaja.* Baja Norte, Mexico: Mexicali Press.

Logic, I. L., & Fisher, R. A. (1923). An inductive paradox: Why even logical null hypotheses cannot be accepted. *Royal Journal of the Royal Statistical Association, 19,* 1–178.

Malgady, R. G., Rogler, L. H., & Costantino, G. (1990). Hero/heroine modeling for Puerto Rican adolescents. *Journal of Consulting and Consulting Psychology, 58,* 469–474.

National Institute of Mental Health. (1976). *Humane procedures for protection of humane subjects.* Rockyville, MD: Author.

Rodriguez, O. (1987). *Hispanics and human services: Help-seeking in the inner city.* Bronx, NY: Fordham University.

Rogler, L. H., Malgady, R. G., Costantino, G., & Blumenthal, R. (1987). What does culturally sensitive mental health services mean? We don't know. *American Psychologist, 42,* 565–570.

Rogler, L. H., Malgady, R. G., & Rodriguez, O. (1989). *Hispanics and mental health: A framework for research.* Melbourne, FL: Krieger.

Shapiro, J., Shapiro, J., & Gonzalez, J. J. (1986). Theory and practice of family group therapy with Hispanic individuals. *Multi-Ethnic Professional Psychology, 6,* iii–122.

Sue, S. (1988). Psychotherapeutic services for ethnic minorities. *American Psychologist, 43,* 301–308.

Social Quagmire Theory: Optimizing Experimental Outcomes by Keeping Research Designs Simple

John M. Wilson, M.Ed.

As is true for most things in life, the Social Quagmire Theory is easy to understand but not easy to apply. In essence, the theory states that all social efforts are doomed to failure because people are involved; the more people, the less functional their efforts. With this basic assumption in mind, the author has attempted to formulate this paper with a minimum of authorship. After several false starts with no authors at all, it was finally decided (by the author) that the author should be the author, as it became rapidly apparent that, although having no author did indeed improve the understandability of the concept, it did little to actually get the paper written. Or, in mathematical terms, there seems to be an absolute number of persons involved in any given social project ($n = 1$) below which one cannot go without experiencing diminishing returns.

Simply stated, social quagmire means that anything people try to do they cannot. Conversely, when people do not try to do something, it is likely to go much better than if they (people) become involved. Thus, random number tables are not really random because people made them up. Even computer-generated random number tables are not truly random because someone had to program the computer. However, there are ways around this problem, if one is willing to accept two critical hypotheses.

Two Critical Hypotheses

The first hypothesis with which we shall concern ourselves is the *Non-Null Hypothesis*. In this instance, an activity should be *almost*

145

embarked upon (to fool the forces of entropy) and then, at the last moment, abandoned (much in the manner of a Hollywood movie that loses its funding at the last minute). In this way, the vectors typically applied by social quagmire (hereafter called "Quags") will be distractedly focused on the activity (called the "dummy load") and unavailable to interfere with our about-to-be-embarked-upon activity (called the "real activity"). Just as the astute reader will become confused when trying to keep these concepts straight, so too will the Quags become disoriented, bumping into one another in a most amusing fashion. The real activity can then be embarked upon and completed before the Quags can regroup.

The second hypothesis is the *Anti-Null Hypothesis*. Here, the activity to be performed is not performed, but life goes on as if it had been performed. For example, a social scientist reports the results of a research project that has not been undertaken as though the experiment had been completed. (The keen-minded reader will ask, "How does this differ from the majority of research presently published?" The author has no ready answer to this query.)

Conclusions

Given that most experimental designs are flawed, few studies are replicable, and very few researchers are willing to attempt replications of others' work, experimentation is much more cost-effective if conducted using the author's strategy. Social scientists closely adhering to the two critical hypotheses introduced in this paper will find their own productivity in the laboratory significantly increased. Those of higher ethical development than the author may even opt to publish one real article for every four to which the one or the other of the two critical hypotheses have been applied. Of course, the author has a jump on other researchers—he now has one publication under his belt.

New Linguistic Weapons in the Quest for the Wholly-Funded Grant

Betty R. Yung, Ph.D.

Wright State University

THE MODERN SEARCH for grant treasure can be compared to the knight's quest for the Holy Grail. Look at the similarity between the two campaigns. Knights are spent through exhausting journeys via foot or horseback as they travel in pursuit of their objective. Nights are spent by grant seekers in the exhausting writing of objectives via word processors. For both, the stakes are high, the battle fierce, and the prize elusive. Poor performance of knightly rites can mean losing the hand of the fair maiden or even loss of life. Poor performance of grantsmanship (w)rites can mean losing the approval of the Dean and hope for promotion and tenure. Thus, both the knight and grant writer fervently quest again and again for the cherished aim. The weapons of the two crusaders are linguistically similar. Knights use swords, whereas grant applicants, because of the rigid page limits set forth by such grail givers as NIMH and NSF, are forced to save previous space by striking the *s* and using only words. Other similarities are summarized in Table 1.

There is one crucial difference between these two soldiers. It is good for the knight to right wrong, but bad for the grantsperson to write wrong. This article is intended to sharpen the (s)words of the contemporary grail seeker with an up-to-date linguistic grindstone.

First, make the prefix **inter** part of your word arsenal.[1] Most grant givers want to be convinced that you will maximize the use of their

---

[1] Do not, however, combine this prefix with **disciplinary.** While the concept of broadening perspective through multi-field input is not outmoded, the term **interdisciplinary** is a little dated. Instead, use **cross-** or **trans-**.

147

TABLE 1. Similarities Between Knights and Grant Writers in Seeking Grant Treasure

Characteristics of Knight	Characteristics of Grant Writer
Lives in castle	Lives in ivory tower
Sits at round table	Sits in at round table discussions
Wears heavy metal	Listens to heavy metal
Uses chainmail	Uses electronic mail
Drinks mead	Uses Mead paper [a]
Worries about beheading	Has B. Heading [b] under control, but worries about overhead
Knightly customs based on chivalry	Nightly customs based on hygiene
Jousts with peers	Undergoes peer review

[a] Contribution of spouse, who works for Mead Corporation.
[b] A. INTRODUCTION
   B. STATEMENT OF NEED

money through the cost-effective fit of your project with key community initiatives and resources. The addition of the term **inter** to such mundane words as **locking, linking,** and **relationships** implies an excruciating level of networking and creates images of appropriately enmeshed and intricate webs.

Second, keep up with the latest linguistic weapons and ruthlessly thrust out the old. This requires eternal vigilance. You should note that **state-of-the-art** is now not; the use of **disadvantaged**[2] can now disadvantage you; and **bottom line** has bottomed out. You must continually question the old and anticipate the new. Is it still acceptable to refer to **resources, user-friendliness,** or **networking**? Will we soon adopt the **seamless solutions** now so prevalent in the business world, their philosophy of **staying close to the customer,** and must we become adept at **exploiting synergies**? It used to be essential to include the term **holistic** in your grant proposal. Such a term would now give you away as an aging warrior. A current imperative is **at risk,** with risk often being qualified to leave no question as to the level of eminent danger (e.g., greatest, highest, multiple, maximum). To prove longevity in battle, the modern word knight might wish to combine two concepts, as in "A

---

[2] Substitute **underclass.**

lack of **holistic** funding places us **at significant risk** for failing in our efforts to (stamp out evil, promote equality and justice, eliminate poverty, etc.)."

These days the use of the term **innovative**—a previously mandated description for all projects—is problematic. Grail dispensers are simply tired of it. However, you place yourself **at risk** of not being funded if you don't convince your funder that you are far and above existing and obviously inadequate and unimaginative ideas and projects. One stratagem you could use is simple thesaurus-browsing; you might choose a devastating synonym from the following armory: **fresh, novel, unique, creative, singular, forward-looking, progressive, advanced, accelerated, landmark, neoteric, uncharted, untrodden, untried, virgin, visionary,** or **promethean.** A recently formed Japanese foundation may have extended the frontier too far by requesting projects that are **dreamful.**

You might wish to consider here the use of another prefix—**hyper**—as in hypermodern or hyperprogressive, although you should recognize that **hyper** can also mean excessive as well as meaning above and beyond. In this regard, you may wish to consider the erudition level and discipline of your reviewers. If you think they may be *Star Wars* fans with fond associations of hyperspace as a mode to get away from Darth Vader, you may be perfectly safe in describing your project as hyperoriginal. If your judges are to be clinical psychologists, who possibly have negative connotations from such terms as hypersensitive and hyperactive, or physicians (e.g., hypertension, hyperthyroidism), you may wish to avoid this qualifier. For clinical psychologists or physicians who also happened to like the movie, it's a judgment call. **Mega** may be a suitable alternative as well, although do not use this to describe the size of the allocation you are seeking. Perhaps the best way to avoid the one-word descriptor problem altogether is the tactic of exaggerated narrative claim. For example, "No one in (the university, the city, the state, the nation, the world, the universe) has conceived of the approach I have developed."

A recent addition to the word pool is **funding streams;** these are frequently described as **poorly coordinated.** The author finds these terms confusing as (a) she is personally unaware of anything other than funding trickles, and (b) she finds the idea of coordinating a stream metaphorically unsound in its representation of a dubious engineering feat.

Modern grants must also speak to the **culturally sensitive** or **culturally specific** nature of their projects. This is relatively easy to work into a human service or biology project (although meanings vary) but is tougher for research grants on functional electrical stimulation.

Contemporary research has noted a correlation between the presence of colons in journal article titles and the fact of publication; there are significantly more articles published with "colonized" titles. This relationship is not true for grant proposal titles. However, one suspects that a similar relationship exists between the clever acronym in a project title and the incidence of funding. Obviously this is a neglected area of research and would represent a worthy subject for grant-funded investigation. The acronym must bear some relationship to the nature of the project, as in a support group for prostitutes, which might be labeled JOHN (Join Our Hooker Network). The only tools required are a thesaurus and a fertile imagination. Purity of heart definitely does not help. One nice aspect of the acronym is that apparently there are no copyrights held in this area, so that acronyms may be repeated (or stolen) between diverse projects. Thus, APT could designate either a vague metaphysical investigation (Abstruse Phenomenological Theories) or a new mode of animal training (Applied Parrot Tickling).

Although you have wielded language as sharp and modern as a laser, do not ignore the traditional elements that are indispensable for fundability. You must emphasize the **comprehensive, systematic, integrated, methodical, carefully coordinated,** but yet **flexible** nature of your project. You must attest to the **grave** and **consequential** problems and needs you are addressing. Your plan, of course, has to have been developed on the **latest research-based knowledge.** Your outcomes should be unfailingly **concrete** and **measurable.** You must verify that you have designed an exhaustive, no-stone-left-unturned **evaluation plan** that will aid in shaping your **pilot** into a **replicable model** or in forwarding reams of **publishable research products** to eagerly awaiting editors. You may feel a lack of originality in making these assurances, but consider the ill fate of the arrogant knight/investigators who asserted:

> Our efforts will be fragmented, as we have chosen a piecemeal approach to address a problem of little significance. We intend

to be conservative and rigid in our methodology, have given no thought as to potential alliances and partnerships, and are extremely amused by the notion of assessment.

Remember: Grantly traditions are as sacred and binding as those of chivalry. Failure to adhere to these conventions will mean no grant-generated money to travel to them.

9

Statistics

A Beginner's Guide to More Significant Statistical Terms in the Psychological Literature

Dennis McDougall, Ed.D., and
Maria de Lalinguastata, Ed.D.

Lewis-Clark State College

As FEINGOLD (1988) noted in his now classic "Beginner's Guide to Statistical Terms," students (like the results of many studies) become confounded quite frequently by statisticalese used in textbooks, journals, and lectures. Feingold provided examples of commonly misinterpreted terms and clarified differences between technical meanings and novices' misguided interpretations of these terms. The present authors identify here additional confusing terms that merit further clarification, particularly for students and nascent members of the scientific community.

1. The "double median test" is not utilized by the Department of Motor Vehicles. "Monotonicity" does not predict future success or failure as a singer. "Confidence intervals" are not periods in one's life when "you just can't lose." And a "Q-sort" is not a reliable procedure for identifying individuals with a penchant for cross-dressing.

2. "Beta weight" is not the goal of Richard Simmons' most recent video weightloss program. "Discrete" variables are no subtler than other variables. And it is a mistake to have less faith in "marginal probabilities" than in probabilities computed elsewhere.

3. Contrary to rumors, scholars do not avoid "bivariate" data. In

155

fact, most scholars become involved with both univariate and bivariate data and may prefer the latter because bivariates are said to be more sophisticated than univariates. Moreover, "binomial distributions" are just as likely to exist in any American community as they are in San Francisco or New York City.

4. "Regression toward the mean" is a phenomenon related to probability and the Central Limit Theorem. It does not refer to the human tendency to become nasty or childish when faced with adversity.

5. A scholar who exclaims, "Tukey! Tukey!" probably is citing a statistical source, rather than imitating an infamous flying creature.

6. "Internal consistency" is a form of reliability. It does not refer to regular bowel movements as influenced by dietary factors.

7. A "standard deviation" is a linear measure of dispersion. It does not refer to (a) a typical weirdo, (b) the annual family vacation at Disneyland, (c) dancing entertainment that accompanies many business lunches, (d) what occurs during adolescence, menopause, or mid-life crises, or (e) questionable sexual acts that most everybody performs at some time or another.

8. In statistics, "non-random assignment" is illustrated by the instructor's tendency to assign, for homework, only the problems from the text that do not have answers provided in the appendix.

9. "Monte Carlo studies" investigate neither the functioning of casinos nor late-model automobiles made by Chevrolet.

10. An "item discrimination index" provides a measure of reliability; it does not quantify the degree to which test items are selected by an instructor to "pick on" particular groups of students.

11. "Spearman's rho" does not refer to the dilapidated portion of a city now occupied only by prostitutes, retired fishermen, and "other shady or salty types."

12. "Goodness of fit" does not refer to (a) the primary criterion used when purchasing blue jeans, or (b) a doctor's guideline used when setting fractured bones (i.e., "crossbreaks").

13. "Venn diagrams," which are helpful in solving probability problems, should not be confused with similar sounding birth control devices, which are helpful in solving other union and intersection problems.

14. "Pearson's r" and other measures of relations express the extent to which ordered pairs vary concomitantly. This applies to statistical, not marital, relations.

15. "Sampling variance" is not an indication of an individual's willingness to try new foods or explore new cultures.

16. Contrary to statistics professors' claims, the "standard error" in statistics does not refer to typical student behaviors such as (a) cramming, (b) "just skimming" assigned readings, or (c) failing to complete sample problems.

17. "Canonical correlation" does not refer to relatives residing in the Vatican, or in monasteries or convents. And, the term "IPSATIVE" does not refer to the new, improved, and expanded version of a popular college entrance exam.

18. In statistics, time-series data frequently demonstrate "serial dependence." This term should not be confused with many children's breakfast-time addiction to sugar-coated substances.

References

Feingold, A. (1988). A beginner's guide to statistical terms in the psychological literature. *Journal of Polymorphous Perversity, 5* (2), 9–10.

Last Chance Statistics for Untenured Professors: An Introduction to the History and Application of Cognitive Psychotherapy to Assumptions Regarding Statistical Hypotheses Testing

William G. McCown, Ph.D.

Institute for the Creative Application of Innovative Statistical Procedure

Judith Johnson, Ph.D.

New School for Antisocial Research

Z. Harry Galina, Ph.D.

Department of Psychological Turmoil

Introduction

The Cognitive Revolution in Statistics: Propitious Hypotheses Testing

Until recently, the average social scientist understood little about the tremendous advances occurring in the nascent branch of statistics known as "propitious hypotheses testing" (PHT). The goal of these new statistical procedures is straightforward: to provide a logical basis for consistent rejection of the null hypotheses (H_0), thereby, at last, maximizing the probability that psychological theory can be grounded in

This paper is humbly dedicated to the memory of the late Sir Cyril Burt (1905–1974).

acceptable empirical findings. Furthermore, despite their theoretical complexity, the methods associated with such a lofty task are also intuitively understandable; they simply involve an application of scientific techniques of cognitive psychotherapy to the assumptions underlying inferential statistical procedures.

Like the paradigmatic revolutions caused by other applications of cognitive psychology, in areas as diverse as learning, social psychology, and artificial intelligence, this sweepingly new approach has shattered the very foundations of classical strategies for social research. Although those stodgily trained in the generations of "classical" statistical techniques may find PHT methods extraordinary, the application of cognitive psychotherapy to statistical procedures promises to spawn the most productive period in the young history of social sciences. Prior to a discussion of specific "Last Chance Statistics," as they are popularly known, a brief history of fundamental shifts in paradigms associated with the philosophical development of cognitive modification of empirical findings is necessary, in order that the nonmathematically inclined reader may make most appropriate use of the numerous techniques of auspicious hypotheses inquiry.

A Brief History of the Cognitive Revolution in Statistics

The roots of this cognitive revolution in statistics can be traced to the prevalence of a Kantian model of data analysis (Kant, 1828/1989). It is a little known fact that Kant, after his failure to secure tenure at Leipzig,[1] radically departed in his philosophical thinking from an emphasis on epistemology and morality to one of statistical inference. (During this period he also began writing romance novels.) Similarly, Freud (1928) was a firm believer in the Kantian notion of categorical *verstehen,* a concept he apparently encountered while reading some of Kant's later, more amorous efforts. A strong case can be made that Freud, too, was a pioneer in the use of cognitive expectations to maximize the power of qualitative data. The actual term "cognitive statistics" was first popularized by Murray (1938), in response to the failure of traditional par-

---

[1] In his classic work "Prologommena to Any Tenure Track" Kant established his famous categorical imperative, "Categorically, it is imperative that results support the hypotheses."

ametric approaches to support the reliability of the Thematic Apperception Test (TAT). Murray sanguinely noted that, "Since the TAT and other thematic material are projective instruments, the experimenter can also project a reliability onto the testing situation, insofar as he *believes and expects the instrument to be reliable*" (emphasis ours).

Unfortunately, Murray was not sufficiently trained in statistical methods and did not capitalize on his fundamentally different conceptual strategy for improving the reliability of projective instruments by allowing the psychometrician, as well as the patient, an innovative degree of projection. Two further separate developments were necessary before the application of cognitive psychotherapeutic techniques could produce the technology of post hoc data manipulation that is so popular today. Contrary to popular sentiment, these paradigm shifts had nothing to do with the academic ethos regarding the necessity of voluminous publications that coincidentally developed during the same period. Instead, they involved a cognitive psychotherapeutic redefinition of two key notions in traditional statistics, *expected value* and *error variance*.

Albert Ellis and the Notion of Expected Values

Reformulation of the concept of expected value fell to Ellis (1962), the famous cognitive psychotherapist. According to classic statistical theory, the expected value is the mean of a sampling distribution, or mathematically:

Given that a Reinmann Stieltjes integral exists such that

$$g(x) \, dF(x)$$

then the expected value of

$$E(x) = \int x f(x) dx$$

Ellis' genius was the use of cognitive therapy to challenge traditional notions of expectation in expected value. According to Ellis, statistical tests are free to deviate around any mean and assume any value the experimenter wishes them to, simply by the experimenter changing his expectations about what the results "should" be. Assumptions of "biased" and "unbiased" population estimators, Ellis claims, reflect the *a priori* cognitive schema of the researcher, and are no more an adequate model of reality than any other particular reality the researcher happens to have embraced (Ellis, 1962). These cognitive distortions can best be remedied by what Ellis calls the ABC model of empirical research: (A) *Always* use the test that supports your hypothesis; (B) *Be* sure to estimate population parameters in line with your hypothesis; and (C) *Correct* error variance for what you need it to be, since such errors are cognitive distortions that interfere with your happiness and publication record. Mathematically, this can be expressed as a simple corollary to the central limit theorem as seen below.

$$E\Sigma(X) = A \text{ Publishable Result}$$

where X is any study, and A Publishable Result is any result that would be accepted by any editor in a refereed journal.

Additional steps (see Harmann, 1968, for proof) demonstrate that this equation is equivalent to the following:

$$\Sigma E\Sigma(X)^{1 \to \infty} = \text{Tenure!}$$

This simple formula indicates that a summation of expected value studies that are publishable will eventually lead to permanent employment, usually defined as "tenure."

The Cognitive Rethinking of Error Variance

A separate development in what are now known as "invasive statistics" was a cognitive reformulation of the notion of error variance. In traditional data analysis, a particular result is thought to be "significant" if the probability of its occurrence or relation with another variable exceeds a particular and admittedly arbitrary level, usually .05. To test this, a similar procedure is followed. For example, in testing the hypotheses that two variables significantly differ in their mean values, independent random samples are drawn from the populations to be compared, and the sampling distribution of this ratio of two independent unbiased estimates of population variance is compared to a known distribution.

Unfortunately, there is always the problem of error variance, caused by random fluctuations, data mistakes, lapses in experimenter attention and the like, which may serve to depress the critical comparison of the observed distribution ratio to that of the known distribution. Basically, this means that if you have more within group variance due to extraneous factors (i.e., more junk in the denominator) you are less likely to find significant results than if you had conducted your experiments in a Candide-like, best-of-all-possible worlds. As a result, a serious shortcoming in traditional statistics is that the experimenter is often faced with a set of findings that *may merely have the appearance* of nonsignificance. The experimenter who fails to find between-group differences where they have been expected by a carefully crafted theory often *knows* that inflated error variance is the culprit. But how can he or she prove this to the scientific community?

Since Kant, however, philosophical arguments have suggested that estimates of error variance should be congruent with the experimenter's expectations. This idea was first represented by Hans Vaihinger, whose book "Statistics as If" was published during Freud's day. Vaihinger was a neo-Kantian admirer of Nietzsche who took the spirit of Kant's and Pascal's ethical doctrine to "behave as if a God exists," and developed it into a statistical method. For Vaihinger, all beliefs were fictions. One man's "error" somehow gained the upper hand and convinced the first party that he was wrong. Applying this to statistical principles, error and true variance are simply convenient fictions that enable us to understand the world. Mathematically, then, Vaihinger redefined error variance as

$$\Sigma E = X \, Y \, Z$$

where the arbitrary characters X, Y, and Z equal any value necessary for desired results to be significant. Again, this was later shown to equal the following, by now, familiar equation,

$$E \Sigma (X)^{1 \to \infty} = \text{Tenure!}$$

This powerful line of reasoning has fostered development of a number of techniques to attenuate within-group differences, based on calculations of what the experimenter expects them to optimally be. These methods will be discussed below.

The Existential Contribution to Statistical Choice

Although less important mathematically to the development of PHT, or "tenurable" statistical techniques, the contribution of other profound thinkers cannot go unnoticed. This is especially true concerning the Existential/Humanists, such as Boss, Binswanger, and Frankl, all of whom have emphasized the role of choice in statistics, and have served to popularize the notion that traditional statistical tests represent an arbitrary constraint on Free Will and Tenure. For example, Victor Frankl has stated with typical existential clarity and relevance that the decision of *what* one chooses to investigate is much more important than what one actually finds, "insofar as serving to illuminate the ineffability of choice over arbitrary and stifling reality" (Frankl, 1949). Recently, this idea has gained some prominence, especially among graduate students experiencing difficulty in completion of their dissertations.

More directly, Binswanger (1946) has discussed the "nauseating arbitrariness of the analysis of variance." In one of the most moving passages in modern statistical theory, he argues:

> I am a man. I live in the world. I can choose to grasp Being in any statistical approach. I can choose an analysis of variance. Or I can choose a less powerful sign test. Who are you, a mere mortal, ultimately not responsible for my life, to tell me which statistic to use? It is my life, my choices, my beliefs, my grappling with the world. I may even choose to disregard the sterile results of inferential assumptions completely, believing instead in my own struggling experience facing the ever present reality of the death that is certain if I do not publish *(Keintenureheit)*. Indeed, I may wish, as a man led to the gallows wishes, to utilize my own, subjective, "last chance statistics" *(Lastchanznumerren)*.

Last Chance Statistics: A Primer of Techniques

Having suggested a firm philosophical basis for development of an alternative paradigm to classical inferential statistics, it is now time to highlight but a few of the many recent developments in this burgeoning field of applied and "results-friendly" data analysis. The current popularity of the cognitive PHT, or so-called "last chance statistics," is evidenced by the large number of computer programs commercially available to assist the user with the procedures commonly known as Post Hoc data manipulation. Such programs include SPPS (Statistics for the Publish or Perish Scientist), BPDQ (Better Publish Damn Quick), and ASS (Adjustments for Social Statistics). Deserving historical note is the early effort "Many Tabs," a program that generated large numbers of correlation coefficients between current restaurant bills and dissertation data, and resulted in some of the most important doctoral theses of the previous generation.

The interested reader is urged to consult Crook and Shambles' (1979) *Quasi-statistic Tests: Post Hoc Manipulation of the Dependent Variable* for a full discussion of the underlying mathematics involved in many of these promising and exhilarating methods of maximizing the probability of H_1. Below are synopses of some of the most popular "last chance statistics," which despite their controversy should prove quite popular for untenured faculty, students struggling with theses, individuals interested in securing grant support, and Republicans documenting the positive effects of trickle-down theory on domestic poverty.

Last Chance Tests Reducing Unexpected Bias

In classical statistics, it can be shown that the expected value of the sample mean is the population mean. This value is called an *unbiased estimate* of a population, because, in the long run, it will equal the population parameter. This handy fact makes all sorts of inferences about broad populations possible from sampling of small portions, and furthermore, allows us to state our degree of certainty in our results mathematically.

As in traditional statistics, the Last Chance Tests assume that unless the sampling mean is equivalent to the expected population value, the sampling mean is also clearly a biased statistic. However, as we have seen, according to cognitive theory of statistical expectancies, the population mean can be thought—quite literally—to be whatever value the experimenter wishes. Therefore, when the experimenter changes his or her cognitive expectancies, he or she is also changing the degree of unbiasness in the sample statistic. Consequently, a perfectly unbiased (in traditional statistics) sample mean may be tremendously biased for the cognitive statistician.

This dreadful condition occurs frequently when the actual data collected are not sufficiently robust to withstand the realities superimposed by the researcher to support the researcher's hypotheses. In this situation, application of traditional statistical tests will almost always be insensitive to the cognitive determinants operating to unconstrain results. This statistical artifact is often known as the problem of "inelastic" or "vanillaed" (compared with "fudged") data. However, since our sample estimate is in fact biased, (i.e., it will not equal what the experimenter expects in the long run) procedures are available for reducing partiality of this number. Among the most popular and simple statistical procedures of this class is the Unbiased Means Elimination Test (Haize, 1971). This procedure relies nicely on Ellis' notion of expectation. Since the population parameter has been "expected" by the experimenter, the Unbiased Means Elimination Test is a procedure to transform the data into the expected sample values that the researcher "has in mind."[2] This is done most often by simply throwing out values that are not in line with the predicted hypothesis. The computer package GLUM (Generally Limit Unmarketable Material) is especially useful for finding experimental values that are not in the expectancy range and removing them with a pseudo-random algorithm.

Another procedure in this class is the Students post hoc t (Wino, 1981). It is simple in its brilliance. Variables that might differ between two groups are examined with a t test. Differences that are significant are published. Those that are not can become "unexpected, biased estimators," and consequently ignored. Mathematically, this procedure is rather simple.

$$E(X) = WHOOPIE!!!$$

---

[2] A sensible point was made by Carl Sagan: One should always remember that since the arrows of time can point either forward or backward, the experimenter may simply choose to work backwards, i.e., if the results don't fit your cognitive set, change your cognitive set (read: hypothesis) to fit the data. Since Einstein was allowed to conduct his "thought" experiments, then why can't untenured professors say, "Gee, I thought it was okay to remove outliers."

This method is very popular with people who do field research, for obvious reasons, especially if they are grant funded.

A useful version of this test, where homogeneity of variance is not assured in the different groups, allows the experimenter to *estimate* an error term, based on his or her expected values, as well as past experiences. For example, an experimenter can rationally set the error term to what it *should have been* if he or she had adequate funding, sufficient lab space, a decent graduate assistant, or a spouse that did not snore. This "estimated unbiased mean" is then used as an appropriate pooled variance, much as the more traditional pooled-variance *t* test. Often the results produce a massive reduction in Type II error.

Modified Bonferroni Adjustments

One of our favorite types of tests is the family of procedures known as the Modified Bonferroni Adjustments (MBAs—also very popular with individuals with this degree). In traditional classical statistics, Bonferroni adjusted *alpha* levels are considered *procedure-wise* to prevent inflation of the possibility of Type I error, or the possibility that the theory is not true but that the results are significant by chance. For example, if during one procedure, 20 experiments are performed, then the *alpha* level in a Bonferroni adjustment would be divided by the number of experiments (in this case .05 / 20, or .0025) to prevent multiple tests causing chance results.

However, as cognitive psychotherapists would tell us, this procedure "catastrophizes" or expects the worse. Why not be more optimistic? Why not maximize the chance that the theory is true? You're going to have statistical imprecision somewhere, and cognitive therapy, along with a heavy dose of existentialism, suggests you choose what is to your advantage. The popular method for this is the Modified Bonferroni procedures, tests which adjust *alpha* levels to maximize the chance that the merely arbitrary model of reality suggested by data may be found to coincide with the reality of adequate theory and expectation.

One procedure, the so-called Turkey's Honestly Insignificant Difference Test, multiplies the *alpha* level by the number of tests employed. In other words, if the experimenter tests 20 hypotheses, the accepted *alpha* level for any of them is 1.0, or any finding at all. The reader is cautioned regarding this method, as its mathematical assumptions are not well developed.

A more desirable approach adjusts the *alpha* levels according to the number of hypotheses that are *expected* to be significant. Since hypotheses would not be tested unless there was a belief that at least some of them were significant, this seems to be a reasonable procedure. Why else would the experimenter have gone to the trouble? If the experimenter tests six hypotheses and thinks three will be significant, he or she can set the *alpha* level at .15, or 3 X .05. Obviously, in this case, individuals who do multihypothetical research are not penalized as they might be under traditional statistical procedures. A further advantage is that it can be mathematically shown that the researcher does not even need to perform *any* experiments whatsoever, as long as he or she expects enough hypotheses to be significant. The tremendous savings in cost implied with this technique add to its attractiveness.

The logic behind this method can also be utilized with a traditional analysis of variance, or ANOVA. One popular procedure is known as the *Shiftless F* test, or simply, an *Adjusted F*. Procedurally, it is accomplished by dividing the bottom term in the analysis of variance by a constant term. When this latter, more conservative procedure is employed, it is referred to as a *Fixed Reduction Analysis Under the Denominator* (FRAUD) *F* test and usually lacks the power of other invasive statistics.[3]

Finally, the researcher may choose the Bonferroni Ordinary Significance Test. This statistical procedure is intuitively appealing and elegant in its design. Kerk (1984) discussed the rationale:

> This test simply allows the experimenter to adjust his/her alpha level for ordinary day-to-day levels of significance. Is .05, or 1 chance in 20, an unreasonable criterion? How often during a day do *you* demand such a proof? Would you cheat

---

[3] As Steven Gould (1988) has noted, "If Heisenberg was allowed to be uncertain about his data and then allowed to plead relative as opposed to absolute reality (and, in fact be awarded the 1932 Nobel), then it is entirely feasible that the untenured professor could be equally justified in post hoc uncertainty about his own results."

on your spouse or run a red light if the chances were 1 in 20
that you would be caught? How about 1 in 5? Come on folks,
let's introduce some reality into our statistics . . .

To perform this test, the experimenter simply chooses whatever
alpha level will be proof enough for him or her. Current debate in the
literature is attempting to clarify whether this choice can be legitimately
made *post hoc* or not. However, if the *alpha* level is sufficiently high *a
priori* (i.e., unity), this concern is irrelevant. Mathematically, this can
be expressed as:

$$E(X) = \frac{\text{Don't Worry}}{\text{Be Happy}}$$

where *alpha* = 1.00, and X is the result of any laboratory finding.

Conclusion

The new techniques of the cognitive statistical revolution are just
being developed. With this in mind, it should be recognized that the
next few years in the social sciences will produce some of the most
interesting and democratic findings our discipline has seen. Theory has
frequently suffered at the hands of the outrageous demands of data. The
untenured professor is now statistically equipped to boldly declare this
liberating message: When theory and data collide, God help the data.
Clearly, however, urgent work (and increased funding) is needed to
develop solutions to determine who indeed will qualify for college tenure once these methods of propitious hypotheses testing become more
commonplace and academic publications become more numerous.[4]

---

[4] Already, a number of intriguing methods have been suggested to solve this
impending crisis. These include random assignment of tenure track employment
throughout the population through some sort of lottery system, perhaps as a
consolation prize (California Lottery Commission, 1989), or the use of meta-
analyses to promote untenured professors with the biggest "effect size" associated with their statistical findings. This procedure has been advocated by the
sociobiologists (Wilson, 1982).

References

Binswanger, Z. (1946). *Dassein statistics*. Studdgartd: Flatus Press.

Boss, Z. (1962). *Boss statistics*. Asbury Park, NJ: Bruce Springsteen Press.

California Lottery Commission. (1989). *A prospectus for using Lotto for assignment of tenured academic positions to guarantee equality of career opportunity*. Freemont, CA: SPSSI Press.

Crook, Z., & Shambles, Z. (1979). *Quasi-statistic tests: Post Hoc manipulation of the dependent variable*. Topeka, KS: Necromancer Press.

Ellis, Z. (1962). *Goddamn it cognitive therapy cures everything and if you don't like it, you're thinking's f***ed*. Dubuque: Impertinence Press.

Frankl, Z. (1949). *Choose it or loose it*. Palco, KS: Onesizefitsall.

Freud, Z. (1928). Statistics as a form of analytic resistance. In Z. Freud (Ed.), *Analysis and H_0*. Hohokus, NJ: Van Nostradamus.

Gould, S. (1988). *The mismeasure of Steven Gould*. Los Angeles: John Holmes Press.

Harmann, D. (1968). *The benzodiazepine statistics*. Washington, DC: American Psychiatric Association.

Haize, Z. (1971). *Invasive statistics*. Yoruba, CA: Epidydimus Press.

Kant, I. (1989). *The romantic writings of Immanuel Kant*. Tubingen, Germany: Harlequin Press. (Original work published 1828).

Kerk, Z. (1984). *Experimental malign*. Harrisburg, PA: Three Mile Press.

Murray, Z. (1938). *How to show pictures to your friends*. Rochester, NY: Kodak.

Sagan, C. (1989). *Clever things I've said about science*. Boston: Clever Carl Press.

Turkey, Z. (1981). *LSD statistics*. Bayou Lafousch, LA: Bilgewater Press.

Vaihinger, A. (1927). *Statistics as If*. Washington, DC: American Enterprise Institute. (Republished, 1985).

Watts, A. (1971). *The Tao of statistics*. Nirvana: Vishnu-with-you Press.

Wilson, E. (1982). Vulgar things academics and prepubescents do in common. In E. Wilson & Q. Herrnstein (Eds.), *The sociobiology of academics*. Fleabag, CT: Social Darwin Press.

Wino, Z. (1981). *Sadistical principles in research design*. Uterp, WY: Prostate Press.

10

Psychology
in
Advertising

Unpredictable.

¶I met her downtown at a Vorpel Gallery opening. (I was invited, she crashed.) Dressed in red—the color of a fire truck—she was meant to start fires, not to put them out. I could hear her laughter from across the room. Everyone could. Her presence drew me to her. Like a moth to a

Intense.

fatal flame. Enticing. Consuming. She left soon after arriving, quickly bored and I by her side. We escaped into the darkness of her loft. We drank. We danced. We thrilled to the night until Dawn—her former bisexual lover and current roommate—objected to the noise. Passionate and reckless, she threatened to punch out

Reckless.

Dawn's lights. ¶It was a stormy relationship. She was a rollercoaster of emotion. Quick to tears. Then to laughter. I was the best thing in her life. I was the worst. It was hard to keep up with her. She was a whirlwind of activity. Shopping. Drinking. Partying. More shopping. The sex

Provocative.

was good. Actually, it was great. Until I found her in bed with another man and a woman. She was just having fun, she said. She told me she loved me so much she would kill herself (after killing me) if I ever tried to leave her. She was so emotional, so provocative. Never dull.

Passionate.

¶I guess you could say she was a BORDERLINE™ woman.

BORDERLINE

Calvin Kline

Concept, design, & advertising copy: Glenn C. Ellenbogen, Ph.D.

Photography: Donna Lynn Brophy

11

Contemporary
Issues
in
Psychology

Advances in the Marketing of Psychological Services and Products

S. David Lee

Buffalo State College

As a psychology undergraduate in my seventh year of study, I have had more than ample time and opportunity to familiarize myself with current trends in the field. A fundamental stumbling block in psychology is that, no matter how much you enjoy the study of human behavior, unless you can manage to earn some money at it your relationship with your landlord is doomed. The question becomes how do you go about supporting yourself in psychology, how do you ensure financial success after obtaining the hard-earned doctoral degree?

The key concept here is "marketing." The goal is to significantly increase your income as quickly as possible. The strategy? Recommend expensive psychological hardware and services that only *you* are able to supply to your vulnerable and easily led clients—at a profit margin that would make an OPEC oil minister gasp in disbelief. Below, you will find a list of potentially lucrative products and services, along with handy advertising copy, guaranteed to bring in those all-important psychology bucks.

Designer clothing for manic personalities and hebephrenic schizophrenics. Colors! Colors! Colors! Styles and combinations never before seen in nature!

Sybyline™ make-up. An exciting line of make-up for the multi-faceted and multi-personality woman.

A complete accessory line. A crown of thorns for those clients with religious delusions. Special 12″ x 18″ MedicAlert tags for hypochondriacs. Stylish sunglasses with mirroring on the interior of the lenses for narcissistic personality disorders. Break-away belts and ties for the indecisive suicidal patient. Clear vinyl underwear for the semi-functional exhibitionist. Monochromatic mood rings for depressives.

Anti-radiation garments for paranoid schizophrenics. Hats and other clothing lined with aluminum foil for daily use and special lead lining for the exclusive line of evening wear.

A 1-900 telephone number featuring a recording that provides clients with the details of the government conspiracy to steal their toothbrushes and to force their pets into revealing the embarrassing details of their owners' sex lives on national television.

Mommy and Daddy blow-up dolls for that final resolution of the Oedipal complex. Let the air out of Daddy and . . .

Throw your voice! This special device fits easily into your mouth and will quickly convince your nonhallucinatory clients that they are indeed hallucinatory, requiring years and years of expensive therapy!

Low-maintenance amusement parks. Lead your unmedicated schizophrenics through an empty "haunted house" and let their delusions and hallucinations do the rest! Turn a hose on your clients as they walk through a drainage conduit and ask them how they enjoyed the Flume Ride. Herd them into a tight group, push them past a small bank of blinking lights as you pick their pockets, and then ask them if they enjoyed the Midway.

A customized line of bumper stickers for schizophrenics.

If You Can Read This, You're An Alien Trying To Steal My Brain Just Like You Did To Elvis

My Other Car Is A Goldfish

Honk If I Am Jesus

President Of The World And Damn Proud Of It!

Guns Don't Kill People—I Do!

War Is Not Healthy For Children And The COMMIES Who INFEST Our Government AND Who Are Hiding IN MY Pockets Stealing!!!!!! My Money So THAT I CAN't Get The new DoNny Osmond ALBUM And hear The SECRET Messages That He's Tryyyyyying To SEnd to Meeeeeeee!

I ♥ Psychotropics

Conclusion

I offer these innovative marketing ideas gratis to the professional/ academic community. My motives are purely altruistic—I seek no recompense of any kind for their use. Of course, a keen-minded professor might just happen to notice that a student who is able to generate such a plethora of creative ideas, present them in such a concise and intelligent manner, and is completely willing to have them used without credit, would make a *very* valuable graduate student, indeed.

Transitional Living: A Terminal Plan[1]

James M. Shulman, Ph.D., and Michael Brickey, Ph.D.

DEINSTITUTIONALIZATION OF MENTALLY ILL and mentally retarded patients has only been partially successful. There are several reasons including lack of funding for transitional or group homes, lack of community acceptance of these facilities, and "culture shock" at the transition from an institutional atmosphere to a homelike atmosphere. Many homeless people are believed to be people who have been deinstitutionalized or who would have been institutionalized by standards a decade ago.

After carefully studying various cost-effective, socially acceptable approaches to solving the problem of providing shelter for those not able to care for themselves, we have discovered an obvious resource that has been overlooked—bus terminals and bus stations. Deinstitutionalized people blend in well with city bus patrons. Like many bus patrons, they often appear tired, lethargic, anxious, apprehensive, and both groups can be found pacing in anticipation. Those who neglect dress or personal hygiene can still fit in with bedraggled intercity travelers. The general chaos, crowded waiting rooms, frequently incomprehensible public address announcements (reminiscent of doctors being paged), day treatment atmosphere of the terminals, nervous chain smoking and coffee drinking, and even the smell of disinfectant mopped floors all contribute to a comfortable, safe, and familiar milieu. Bus terminals are usually located downtown, which makes them convenient for patients who can walk to local social agency offices or, if they prefer, can meld into the bustling crowds without being harassed by police officers. Institutional food has always had a bad reputation and deinstitutionalized people speak highly of the franchise and vending machine foods avail-

---

[1] With acknowledgment to Jonathan Swift's Modest Proposal essay (1729).

able 24 hours a day. Coffee and cigarettes are available around the clock.

Though vacations would normally be difficult to manage without one-to-one supervision, patrons would only need to save the price of a bus ticket from disability or welfare checks, or from pan handling, to be able to visit bus stations in other towns. This possibility offers the ideal vacation—a combination of being in a place different and yet familiar. Some patrons complain of having to pay money to watch television on the coin operated televisions, but others are pleased that the televisions work and that they can choose the channels. For vocational rehabilitation, bus stations offer entry level employment in package handling, express mail, porter, food service, and janitorial jobs.

The economics of the "terminal plan" are especially appealing. Bus stations are already in existence and they are often underutilized. Therefore, housing is not needed as the institutional seating at stations, in addition to abundant floor space, offer ample room for patients to sleep. Thus there is no need to worry about capital expenditures, zoning hassles, or start-up lag times. It would be helpful to have showers in rest rooms (as some terminals already have). Extra revenues could be generated by making the showers coin operated. The shower service would benefit both deinstitutionalized people and weary travelers.

There are some potential problems with this plan. Unscrupulous vendors would know when disability checks were issued and they might take advantage of patrons. To mitigate this problem and to assure steady business, the fast food franchises might be mandated to offer monthly meal tickets and/or accept food stamps. The increased business volume might even create more competition and, consequently, lower prices. Locker rentals could be made available on a monthly basis and the fees withdrawn automatically from patients' checks. Ticket agents could advise patrons about overcrowding in other stations, particularly for those going south for the winter. An LPN might be assigned to each terminal to administer medications from a ticket window.

Though downtown bus terminals offer the ideal location, suburban locations might also be useful. With downtown parking becoming scarcer and more expensive, suburbanites would welcome bus transportation services and terminals in their communities. The additional utilization by deinstitutionalized patrons who want to escape urban living can help justify new suburban stations.

Our proposal comes at a time when Greyhound is under new management which is emphasizing sprucing up bus stations and adding short intercity and suburban routes (Belden, 1989). These changes could mean more and better bus station facilities—and as a result, increased housing potential. We think the advantages of the "terminal plan" are manifold and we are investing our savings in Greyhound stock.

References

Belden, T. (1989, August 6). New departures for Greyhound: The firm is not a dog, chairman insists. *Philadelphia Enquirer,* pp. E-1, E-10.

New Strategies for Psychology Licensure Preparation: The Trivial Pursuit Paradigm

Sally D. Stabb, Ph.D.

Memphis State University

BECOMING A LICENSED psychologist is a post-doctoral hurdle over which new Ph.D.s leap (or attempt to leap) with varying degrees of agitation and preparation. Studying for the licensure exam has become Big Business, with licensure candidates regularly dropping $400 a pop for prepared written or taped materials. Those with time and money to burn, obsessive-compulsive personality disorders, or frequent panic attacks often choose to attend the $800 preparatory course as well. The present article proposes the development and marketing of a cheaper, equally effective (since nothing really prepares you for the real thing anyway), and more fun approach.

The basis for this new study program is the board game "Trivial Pursuit." The inane and arcane bits of "knowledge" required for the original game are resoundingly reminiscent of the details memorized for psychology licensure. Therefore, the board and accompanying materials can be easily modified for this new application. The game will enhance collegial interaction as peers strive to outguess members of the opposite team and plumb the obscurest depths of their mental minutiae to dredge up answers for their own side. Potential licensees will certainly want to play again and again, in a (vain) attempt to "memorize the deck."

As in the original game, the Licensure Trivial Pursuit game will have cards that list various categories. However, instead of History, Geography, and so forth, these categories will correspond to major areas of licensure study. The acronym PESSINC (as in "Oy, what I wouldn't

Psychopharmacology

Eighty percent of American house-wives and their ever-receptive physi-cians will choose Valium as their "minor tranquilizer of choice" this year. The other 20 percent will select what similar drug?

Ethics

You are a psychologist hired by a large corporation to evaluate its managers for promotion/selection to a new position. In the course of your interviews, you discover that one manager has been having bizarre intimate relationships with the custodial parent of a child client of yours. Interestingly, so have you. Your most ethical course of action is?

Social Psychology

If a field-dependent person is given an arousing drug and then placed in a simu-lated bystander behavior enactment with three confederates, two of whom are high on the Mach scale and one who is a naive scientist, the best approach to attitude change would be what?

Statistics and Test Construction

Is Homoscedasticity still a viable DSM-III diagnosis?

Industrial/Organizational

The effects of punk music on job performance and job satisfaction show differential effects depending on the type of band (e.g., "Toxic Lox" vs. "Party-line Junkies"). In what direction(s) are these effects?

Neuropsychology

What obscure neuroscientist discov-ered what stimulation of the medial forebrain bundle (pleasure center) did and why didn't s/he tell us sooner? When will the technology be commercially available to me?

Clinical, Counseling, & Community

Most recent research on the effec-tiveness of pet therapy in Adult Chil-dren of Alcoholics (ACOAs) has de-termined that, in comparison to para-keets, wire-haired fox terriers have a greater impact on what aspect of ACOA recovery?

Figure 1. Sample questions from the Licensure Trivial Pursuit game.

do to be pessinc this exam!'') is a handy mnemonic device for remembering the categories Psychopharmacology (P), Ethics (E), Social Psychology (S), Statistics and Test Construction (S), Industrial/Organizational (I), Neuropsychology (N), and Clinical, Counseling, and Community (C). (See Figure 1 for sample questions from the Licensure Trivial Pursuit game.)

Players move around the Licensure Board in endless circles with no position having any strategic advantage. A player or team wins the game by successfully answering 200 questions—just like the actual licensing exam. However, players may wish to modify the number of answers needed to win to match their state's cutoff scores (e.g., 150 right rather than 200). The distribution of questions per category on the exam is highly erratic—you can expect to have to answer only 2 or 3 questions on Neuropsychology or Psychopharmacology, but be prepared for 50 each in the areas of Ethics, Industrial/Organizational, and Statistics/Test Construction.

If you can't answer the sample questions presented here and hundreds more just like them *right now,* the author suggests that you purchase a playing set of Licensure Trivial Pursuit immediately. Checks, money orders, or cash, in the amount of $75—a mere pittance in comparison to the cost of most other study formats—can be sent directly to the author. Get started right away! You and your other non-licensed colleagues will enjoy hours of tedious questions and answers and revel in the exhausted delirium that only in-depth study can bring about. Order yours today!

Readings

Adventurous, B. (1987). Applied social psychology experiments they never told you about. *Journal of Human Subjects Committee Rejects, 58,* 34–51.

Getcaught, Y. (1988). *Modern ethics for the modern world.* Los Angeles: Slidemore Press.

Kidding, R. U. (1985). Avian vs. canine intervention in the treatment of alcohol co-dependence. *The American Pet Therapist, 3,* 231–240.

Stoned, I. M. (1969). Doctors' favorite drugs and how you can get 'em. *Social Deviants, 23,* 113–119.

Test, F., & Test, T. (1978). Homo- and heteroscedasticity: Reverse discrimination? *Statistics and Social-sexual Policy, 2,* 67–72.

Whiz, G. (1983). What every personnel psychologist should know about loud rock-and-roll music. *Get A Clue, 30,* 90–94.

Yesyesyes, O. (1989). Direct medial forebrain bundle self-stimulation for me, the "old way" for you. Unpublished doctoral dissertation, American Institute of Experimental Pleasures.

Marketing Strategies for the Counseling Professional: Ideas That Make Dollars and Sense

Jerry Spicer, M.H.A.

As EACH DAY PASSES, the future of mental health services becomes more unpredictable. In today's turbulent environment, the professional counselor cannot assume that good intentions, skills, and training will assure survival in the increasingly competitive marketplace. Some, like myself, can sell out and drop anchor in the safe harbor of management. Those of you with stronger personal ethics or lesser psychopathology, however, will continue to sail the rough seas of direct services. But your days are numbered unless you apply the following principles to your business.

The Key to the Future—Creating Demand

Most of us have sat through some seminars on marketing in which we learned about how our economy moved from being a production-oriented (i.e., make it first, then sell it) to a market-driven system where customer needs drive production. But now we are in a new stage—industry no longer *responds* to demand, it actually *creates* it! Today's economy is dependent on the consumption of unnecessary products and services fostered by evermore sophisticated marketing and advertising. How else can we explain tanning booths, designer jeans, and a Republican President?

What is the future of mental health? To survive and prosper, you too must target your customers (anyone with money or insurance) and then convince them that they need *your* help, regardless of their real

187

mental health status. (Some of you will by now be raising irrelevant
questions about ethics and values. If you must berate yourself with
questions of morality, do so in private as a cathartic exercise, but don't
let your concerns stand in the way of achieving the American dream—
big money.)

How to Create Demand

As impoverished professionals, counselors and psychologists lack
the financial resources to wage extensive sales and promotion campaigns, but there are several cost-effective strategies readily available.
The first strategy is *working with allied professionals*. Early in the
development of the legal profession, attorneys discovered the advantages of seeking out other professionals who would direct clients their
way. Today, "ambulance chasing" is a mainstream tactic of legal firms
and it is often taught in law school as a senior level seminar (usually
called something like, "Business Skills for the Entrepreneurial Attor-
ney"). Other examples include crime reporters who establish referral
relationships with homicide detectives and nursing home administrators
whose cousins run the local funeral home. Table 1 lists a sample of
counseling professionals and peers from other professions who could
serve as marketing distribution channels.

In working with other professionals, the counselor has several levels of cross-support to consider. At the simplest level, the counselor and
allied professional hang-out together or *"network."* Interaction is social
with personal friendship, mutual support, gifts, and the occasional bribe
serving to cement the bond. The human relations training and ability to
fake an unconditional positive regard for another person gives the counselor an advantage in forming these strategic relationships.

The second strategy is to go beyond the personal relationship to
create a business partnership with an allied professional. Although this
approach calls for a legal contract with shared economic risk, it also
holds the greatest potential for financial success. The first stage is the
shared business card. For example, one side of the card advertises a
funeral home and printed on the reverse side is the name and telephone
number of a grief counselor. Printing costs are split, and both the mor-
tician and grief counselor distribute cards, potentially doubling their
business. At the second stage the commitment to promotional efforts

TABLE 1. Counseling Specializations Matched to Other Allied Professionals Who Could Act as Referral Sources

Counseling Specializations	Allied Professionals
Adolescent adjustment	Rock stars; anyone under 20
Adult children	Parents
Alcoholism	Bartenders, taxi drivers
Agoraphobia	Mailmen; meter readers; grocery delivery boys
Codependency	World's population
Drug abuse	DEA/FBI agents; police; Manuel Noreiga
Eating disorders	Fry cooks at fast food chains; bakers
Grief therapy	Ambulance, fire, and rescue drivers; hospital/hospice nurses
Learning disorders	Dan Quayle
Marital communications	Ivana Trump
Sexual disorders	Clerks at X-rated video and adult entertainment stores

Note. Counselor is operationally defined as any individuals who have ever been paid for giving advice, or who have thought that their advice was so good that they should have been paid. Professional is determined by a self-assessment questionnaire and includes all persons who have been called, or have called themselves, professional, and who have graduated from, or have ever attended college, or who drive by a college at least once a month. This list is not exhaustive and the reader is encouraged to expand the possible synergistic combinations.

expands with an aggressive campaign of advertising, brochures, and billboards cooperatively developed and funded. (A creative example is a promotion for a sexual addictions counselor in the opening credits of an X-rated video.) The inevitable success at the first two stages leads to the third and highest stage, the joint business venture. Called "vertical integration" by business, this tactic enables the counselor to become a business partner or even to own a related business. Physicians have understood this technique for years, and today's astute doctor owns a few shares in the pharmacy, medical equipment company, or for-profit hospital used. An innovative example is the "hired gun" concept where doctors frustrated with losing revenues to managed care firms set up their own precertification companies, thus receiving as consultant fees those dollars lost in patient care. (Caution: Be aware of various laws regarding restraint of trade and racketeering. The preferred solution is to control most of the market, allowing you to charge high enough prices to hire a good mob lawyer and let him worry about it.) In our previous example, it is only a matter of time until our sexual addictions counselor becomes a silent partner in the company (Back Alley Productions, Inc.) that produces the videos. And the counselor's case files (names deleted, of course, for ethical reasons) hold a wealth of ideas just waiting for cinematic expression! Once begun, the acquisition of related businesses snowballs, as you buy out the competition, selling off its assets to fund a vacation condo in Costa Rica. Another benefit of the joint business venture is that it enables you to attract celebrity sponsors. Thousands of famous people, alive and dead (the latter usually working for lower fees), are available for a small piece of the action to lend their names to your new business. Recently, publicity agents have contacted the author offering these possibilities:

- The Jimmy Swaggert Clinic for Sexual Disorders
- Donald Trump's Marital Counseling Center
- The Elvis Presley Diet Program
- Jim & Tami Bakker's Career Guidance Institute

To illustrate the application of these principles, the following case study from the author's files is offered.

Case Study

John and Mary Cracker are a husband and wife team of professional counselors specializing in bird behavior. Both are of below average intelligence, with unremarkable educations from mediocre schools. They are, however, smart enough to recognize their limitations. The Crackers chose to enter the unlicensed field of psittacine psychology, opening